OUR BODIES,
OUR SOULS

OUR BODIES, OUR SOULS

A Jewish Perspective on Feminine Spirituality

Tziporah Heller

TARGUM/FELDHEIM

First published 2003
Copyright © 2003 by Tziporah Heller
ISBN 1-56871-216-2

Published by:
TARGUM PRESS, INC.
22700 W. Eleven Mile Rd.
Southfield, MI 48034
E-mail: targum@netvision.net.il
Fax: 888-298-9992
www.targum.com

Distributed by:
FELDHEIM PUBLISHERS
202 Airport Executive Park
Nanuet, NY 10954

Printed in Israel

More of Tziporah Heller's work is featured on her website,
www.tziporahheller.com

NEVE·YERUSHALAYIM

נ ו ה · י ר ו ש ל י ם

בס"ד

PRESIDENT
Bernard Hochstein

DEAN
Rabbi Dr. Dovid Refson

DIRECTOR GENERAL
Avrohom Stefansky

NEVE
SCHOOL OF GENERAL
JEWISH STUDIES
Rabbi Moshe Chalkowski

MECHINA
Rabbi Eliezer Liff

SHALHEVET
Rabbi David Kass

ISRAELI DIVISION
Rabbi Chaim Metzger

FRENCH DIVISION
Rabbi Gerard Ackermann

BNOS CHAVA
Rabbi Dovid Abramov
Rabbi Nosson Geisler

MICHLELET ESTHER
Rabbi Boruch Smith
Rabbi Ari Winter

ME'OHR BAIS YAAKOV
Rabbi Zecharya Greenwald

MIDRESHET TEHILLAH
Rabbi Jeremy Kagan

BAIS YAAKOV
SHOSHANIM
Rabbi Kalman Rosen

MAALOT YERUSHALAYIM
Phyllis Geisler

MORESHET INSTITUTE
Rabbi David Kass

FAMILY INSTITUTE AND
COUNSELING CENTER
Dr. Yisrael Levitz

SPEECH AND LANGUAGE
CENTER
Prof. Jerry Koller

MONSEY ACADEMY
FOR GIRLS
Mrs. Rivka Shear

WARM HOME PROJECT
Rabbi Ronald Greenwald

REGISTRAR
Dr. Avraham Schwartzbaum

ASSOCIATE REGISTRAR
David Starr-Glass

ASSOCIATE DIRECTOR
Chaya Wexler

Since 1978, Rebbetzin Tziporah Heller, a truly gifted teacher, has held thousands of Neve Yerushalayim students spellbound by her dramatic and profound lectures. These students recall with gratitude her crucial influence on their spiritual and religious development.

Mrs. Heller's encyclopedic Torah knowledge, the depth of her thought, and her remarkable ability to simplify complex topics and present them with humor, all combine to make her classes memorable. Her warm personality, her humanity, and the attention she manages to pay each individual, always leaves an indelible impression. No less remarkable are her *tzinus*, humility, and self-effacement.

The influence of Rebbetzin Heller is by no means limited to Neve Yerushalayim. Her speaking tours in the United States and Canada, her widely distributed Torah tapes, and her other published works have given many others the opportunity to share her wisdom.

May this book serve to enrich the lives of all those who take its lessons to heart.

Rabbi Dovid Refson, Dean
Neve Yerushalayim College

P. O .Box 43016, Beit Yitzchak Street, Har Nof, Jerusalem, Israel. Tel. (02) 654-4555. Fax (02) 651-9376 neve@neveyerushalayim.org.il
neve@neveyerushalayim.org.il (02) 651-9376 פקס .(02) 654-4555 טלפון .ישראל, ירושלים, הר נוף, בית יצחק רח' 43016 .ת.ד
Neve Academic Office: 25 Broadway, Suite 403, New York, NY 10004. Tel. (212) 422-1110. Fax (212) 785-0898 neve@idt.net
Neve Executive Office: 71 Route 59, Suite 104, Monsey, NY 10952. Tel. (845) 425-9411. Fax (845) 425-9412 schachtel@att.net

ספר זה מוקדש

לזווג יפה

עבור

לאה ברכה בת שרה מירל

Many people's kindness and generosity
have made this book possible.

Some of those who chose to help bring the book
to light chose to remain anonymous.

Among them is a woman of great dignity and
kindness whom I have known since my childhood.

Contents

Introduction

I still recall the day that this book got its start. The summer sun in the park and the children's absorption with the play equipment made sitting down on a bench with a friend one of life's little treasures. Shira Frank was the friend. An eminent therapist, social worker, and author, Shira combines erudition and that rare something called wisdom with one of the warmest hearts I have ever encountered. She is deeply insightful about human nature and the conflicts we tend to encounter nowadays. Shira suggested that the time had come to offer alternatives to women who have no idea of the insights that classical Jewish sources offer. As it turns out, before this book saw the light of day, I was to write a smaller one, *More Precious than Pearls*, in which King Solomon's Woman of Valor is presented to the English-speaking public. However, countless women who are unacquainted with Jewish thought would never see anything King Solomon had to say as relevant to their own lives. What was needed was a book in which both contemporary and traditional values were lucidly presented in order to offer the most elusive of all resources: real choice. Shira provided the inspiration and impetus to begin work on the manuscript, transcribed some of the earliest tapes, and reviewed my work carefully. The credit for this book's eventual emergence lies fully with her.

God has also blessed me with other friends that He has allowed to cross my path. Gila Manolson, author of *The Magic Touch, Outside/Inside,* and *Head to Heart,* and arguably one of the clearest voices in what might be called the women's affirmation movement, transcribed further material, encouraged me to add to it substantially, did some initial editing, and supplied the notes. Sara Rigler, featured writer on the popular Aish.com website and author of many profound yet readable articles on spiritual topics (many of which are included in the book *Heaven on Earth*), did some major reorganization and rewriting, creating a coherent, well-structured manuscript. Sarah Schneider offered many valuable comments, Aliza Bloom made several important suggestions, and Miriam Greenwald painstakingly contributed her editing skills.

My husband, Rabbi Dovid Heller, has shown great forbearance over the years, but this book has got to be the prizewinner in the field of frustration provocation. So much work and time was spent on what might have led to nothing. I would have given up years ago if not for his encouragement.

Human wisdom and efforts go only so far. Torah gives us insight into a world that transcends ours, and offers a glimpse at what believing Jews see as God's reality. If it were not for Torah, there would be no book — and indeed there would be no choices for us as women.

It is my hope that my readers make the choices that lead them to a life that is rewarding and joyous.

One

Feminism or Masculism?

Many women today are torn by inner conflict. For those of us who experience this, the price this conflict exacts in our lives is incalculable.

We hear within ourselves two opposing voices. One calls out to our sense of womanhood. Many of us with families see something of ourselves lost in the reflected image of mother-off-to-work-again in our children's eyes. Sometimes our days end up fragmented into tense mini-dramas, double features such as *The Train That Came Late* and *Who Will Take Him to the Dentist*? At those times we find that "the executive with the report due tomorrow" has the leading role and that the role of mother is forced backstage.

The cliché that all things are possible suddenly rings hollow. The blank check that was presented to women as their ticket to freedom has bounced. To quote Naomi Wolf, "Feminism was undergoing a form of triage. Whatever was inessential got hauled overboard so as not to rock the fragile all-important boat of the new family."

Others of us who have written motherhood and even marriage out of the script altogether often feel the loss in having cut ourselves off from a side of life we sense has great richness. As our potential childbearing years draw to a close, we face with increasing panic the realization that if we do not alter our lives now, one of life's most precious opportunities will be lost forever.

Yet another voice rings in our ears — one warning us that traditional female roles cause slow death by strangulation. A growing number of women who have chosen to delay advancing their careers in order to raise a family are left filled with insecurity and doubt. The motto we jokingly bear on our aprons, "For this I spent four years in college?" (never mind another three in law school), inspires in us less humor than brewing resentment as we question if we have, in fact, "sold out."

In the end, many of us are confused by a host of push-pull emotions, leaving us wondering who we really are and if it is possible that our essence exists in a greater, more eternal vision that has been lost in the shuffle.

We want to be whole. We want it all. We want to be women who are actualizing the full range of our potentials. We should — we were made to strive for completion.

Judaism believes in wholeness, in the valid claims of contrasting aspects: in being part of society while remaining a unique people, in being part of a community while maintaining one's individuality, in being a full-fledged part of the world while also being a woman. Before focusing specifically on the Jewish view of how women can flourish in modern society without experiencing conflict, let us look at contemporary reality.

The Rise and Fall of the Happy Homemaker

Women of the Western world have invested close to half a century in rebelling against the advertising industry's "Happy Homemaker" feminine ideal. The Happy Homemaker was the coiffured blond, ever-smiling, empty-headed female of the '50s and '60s, whose sole pleasures in life were serving the moistest cake possible to her family and having dishes in which she could see her reflection.

The Happy Homemaker was not Jewish. The stereotype she represented was antithetical to the idealized Jewish vision of womanhood, portrayed as early as King Solomon's time in his poem *A Woman of Valor*. He spoke of qualities such as wisdom, courage, creativity, business acumen, and the profound insight needed to relate to individuals according to their specific needs. Nowhere is "lovin' " equated with "somethin' from the oven," as the 1960s Pillsbury ad would have it. Nowhere is housework presented as a goal by which a woman's worth is measured. It is rather a means toward a goal, which is raising a family of exemplary humans as she develops her own spiritual and moral self.

Women's contributions to society have always been far more than physical. The tragedy is that this obvious fact has too often gone unrecognized. Physical nurturing can express caring, but it is only one part of a complex mosaic of personal feminine self-expression. It is a gross distortion to equate this part with the whole.

The Happy Homemaker was not the first woman to understand nurture and feminine self-actualization in such limited terms. Before her time, however, the practical exigencies of life gave household chores greater meaning. In preindustrial society, women were valued – and valued themselves – for their irre-placeable contributions to the functioning of the home. While many women (and men) would have undoubtedly welcomed the opportunity to be freed from some of the tedium involved in their jobs, the importance of the housewife's role was recognized, if for no other reason than because of the absence of machines that could perform the same tasks.

The technological liberation of the homemaker (with the in-ventions and widespread use of gas and electric stoves, washing machines, ready-made clothes, prepared food) left a void. "What do I do with my life now?" wondered those women who desired to contribute something of true value. The answer: "Bake another cake." The Happy Homemaker arrived on the scene as the role model who continued to glow with fulfillment while totally im-mersing herself in dwindling and increasingly meaningless do-mestic chores.

The inevitable result of this was the erosion of whatever sta-tus had hitherto been ascribed to traditional feminine roles. After all, no one could be fooled for long – how important could that cake be? Predictably the Happy Homemaker's baking lost its taste after a generation or two. In the wake of her demise, a new woman was born seeking gratification that could not be found in even the flakiest pie crust. And thus began the wholesale aban-donment of homemaking and even motherhood in favor of occu-pations outside the home that imparted the sense that one was doing something worthwhile. "Feminism," as quickly as it gained momentum, lost its calling as a movement to promote female self-actualization and rapidly atrophied into "careerism."

To add insult to injury, Western society was simultaneously

becoming more and more secularized, so that education of children became increasingly defined in terms of information instead of moral values. If learning history and algebra was more important to a child's development than learning honesty and generosity, then a professional schoolteacher was certainly better equipped to teach than a mother.

Today, more than ever, women's spiritual contributions to home, family, and community are unrecognized not only by men, but, more painfully, by women themselves.

A rabbi I know was speaking on a university campus about the role of the Jewish woman. An angry young woman interrupted his lecture.

"While you're here at the podium lecturing, where's your wife? In the kitchen?"

"My wife is a professional," he answered calmly. "She runs a group home for unwanted children." The woman was taken aback.

"Let me tell you a little about what she does," the rabbi continued. "Her job entails, among other things, overseeing the children's motor and intellectual development, teaching them the social skills they will need to succeed later in life, and helping them to develop a positive, healthy self-image. She accomplishes this, by first creating an environment conducive to spiritual well-being and growth and then designing an individualized approach to meet the unique needs and talents of each child in the home. If these children were left to grow up on the street, they'd have little chance of emerging as happy and productive adults. But thanks to my wife, they will hopefully succeed."

By this time the young woman's fire had cooled. Apparently

she was satisfied that this particular religious wife was indeed doing something valuable with her life.

For a second or so it seemed that the rabbi would continue his talk from where he left off. His basic honesty, however, got the better of him, and he said with a grin, "The truth is that the eight children in the home she runs are ours, and if she didn't want them, who would?"

The blaze returned to the eyes of the disgruntled woman. She had no experience of a society in which there is more to raising a family than baking a cake. This dyed-in-the-wool feminist could understand that raising other people's children required intelligence and creativity, but running one's own home and raising one's own children seemed to her a worthless and unfulfilling vocation.

Another revealing incident happened to me several years ago in Jerusalem. A census taker came to our home. For various reasons, I chose not to participate in the count. My children were in school, and the female census taker found me sitting at the dining-room table surrounded by books, looking very professorial. Over a cup of coffee, I discussed with her, in fluent Hebrew, my philosophical stance. She was interested in the discussion and left at least respecting the intellectual clarity of my position.

The law requires that anyone refusing to take part in the census must be visited again, so a few weeks later she reappeared. In the meantime, of course, she had interviewed hundreds of people, so she did not recognize me from our previous discussion. This time she saw the Friday morning me, surrounded by small children and elbow-deep in challah dough. Sizing up my intellectual capacity with a cursory glance at the scene, she pointed at the paper she held and spoke slowly and clearly in beginner's Hebrew.

"This...is...a...census. A...census...is...when...we...count...people. We...want...to...count...*all*...the...people. Sign...this."

To her, being a mother and housewife obviously precluded any possibility of being an intelligent human being.

The discrediting of women in their traditional roles has led inevitably to a prejudice in favor of manhood that extends across the board. In the end, many of us have succumbed to the pervasive bias that anything men have, do, or are is de facto better and more desirable than what women have, do, or are. Shockingly few of us even pause to question this assumption. Gloria Steinem's wry and accurate observation that "if men could menstruate, it would be a boast-worthy event" in truth reflects not only how men view themselves but how most women view everything male as well. Thus, mainstream feminism should really be called "masculism," because it glorifies everything that pertains to men and seeks to appropriate it for women.

A good example of this mindless masculism is the concept of feminine cigarettes. When Virginia Slims launched itself at the beginning of the feminist movement, its advertising campaign went something like this: Men have oppressed women by withholding from them the right to smoke so that women were forced to smoke in secret. Now a woman can prove her liberated status not only by smoking in public, but by smoking specifically feminine cigarettes, made just for her. The question was never asked: But is smoking good for anyone? Claiming the right to smoke because men have it is like asserting the right to be a kamikaze pilot as an equal job opportunity.

In terms of attitudes toward traditional Judaism, this masculism has proven equally damaging. It has translated into the deeply rooted suspicion that any *mitzvah* (commandment) that pertains to men, such as wearing a *tallit* (prayer shawl), must perforce indicate males' superior religious status and therefore be an enviable privilege. On the other hand, any commandment pertaining to women, such as *mikveh* (ritual immersion), must reflect female inferiority.

In short, in the modern secular vision, the only mode of being that carries status is male. Parents of "liberated" children are more often proud of their daughter's interest in science than of their son's interest in cooking. Many a modern woman wants her husband to share in child-rearing and homemaking, not so that he, too, may experience this enriching part of life, but from her own desire to be free to pursue "more important" things. Being told, "You think (or manage or behave) like a woman" is rarely taken as a compliment, whether the remark is addressed to a male or a female.

As a result, many feel that the only solution is to promote a unisex ideal eliminating any basis for sexism and discrimination. Yet by advocating that equality be achieved by sameness (which usually means making women more like men), society is not dealing with the issue of prejudice against women — it is running away from it.

Being a woman, in the Jewish view, however, is a role that is not only valuable in its own right, but requires intelligence and creativity in all spheres.

Two

Acknowledging Differences

Judaism maintains that God created men and women inherently and nonnegotiably different in specific areas. This contrasts fundamentally with feminism, which insists that, except for the obvious physical distinctions, there are no inherent, but only socialized, divergences between men and women. As proof, traditional feminists point to the biological fact that men and women share 95 percent of the same DNA structure and differ only in one chromosome. The stereotypical thinking in which there is only one gender, and women are merely close to the real thing, dies hard (though some feminist educators such as Paglia do acknowledge now that women are distinct).

In Jewish thought, however, not only do women differ from men physically, emotionally, intellectually, and spiritually, but these differences are beneficial to both sexes. Difference need not imply difference in value. We in the West tend to appraise differences in terms of relative worth: better or worse, prettier or uglier. Judaism maintains that a dog is not worse than a cat because it is less agile, more easily excitable, and takes longer to housebreak, nor is a cat worse than a dog because it is less playful and more aloof. There is an unswerving belief in the integrity of pluralism.

Accordingly, arguments for real differences between the sexes need not engender heated debate over who is better than whom. They need not lead, as they have, to books containing chapters bearing titles such as "The Brain That's Lame Lies Mainly in the Dame," or, in the more recent anti-male backlash, "Men versus Dogs: Some Clear-Cut Comparisons." While the reluctance to recognize gender differences in light of such negative inferences is understandable, denying the true characteristics of our sex forces us to exclude immeasurable opportunities for growth and self-expression. In the end, forfeiting each sex's unique attributes and contributions is too great a price to pay for the sake of "equality." The road to peace in the "war between the sexes" lies, not in either gender's self-negation, but in establishing true mutual respect and appreciation.

Difference Leads to Contribution: Spiritual Ecology at Work

According to Jewish tradition, Adam, the first spiritual mortal being, was originally androgynous, containing within him/herself all aspects of both masculinity and femininity. Hence, in recounting the generations from the Creation, the Torah says, "Male and female He created them...and called their name Adam." The subsequent creation of woman occurred not through forming a new being from scratch, as it were, but through separating the female aspects from this first person.

The original Adam was totally self-sufficient and could even reproduce him/herself. Adam had the mind and body necessary to use the entire world that was at his/her disposal. Nonetheless, God said, "It is not good for Adam to be alone." Why not?

The "not good" quality of existential aloneness has two major aspects. The first is that total independence would invariably lead Adam to view him/herself as an authority similar to God and would thus promote an egocentric, or human-centered, vision of reality. Only the consciousness of being dependent on someone or something outside of oneself allows the vision of a theocentric world to emerge.

The second aspect of the need for the original Adam to experience a division of self was God's desire to create the possibility of far-reaching and meaningful contribution. The world was created so that God could express His primary attribute of *chesed* (loving-kindness). Both men and women were created in order to express the part of themselves that is in God's image. One of the strongest manifestations of our humanity, therefore, is our desire to contribute. Our moments of deepest pleasure come from the feeling of having made a difference. Only with another person could Adam realize his full potential for giving.

But not all giving between people is real giving. Giving means supplying what the other truly requires, not what feels good to give or what one's own emotional agenda dictates. Forcing one's son to attend medical school when he wants to be a carpenter is illusory giving. Sending a son to medical school when he wants to be a doctor and will be a good one is an act of true giving, which always works on the premise of genuine lack.

Instead of just cloning the first human, God divided Adam into two distinct and different people with differences not only in the physical sphere, but on all levels: intellectual, emotional, and spiritual (i.e., the desire to become closer to God). Each therefore genuinely lacked things the other could supply.

Of course, women also differ from one another, as do men, and this reality allows both to give meaningfully to members of their own sex as well. It is when crossing the male-female line, however, that the most dichotomies are found, and therefore it is here that the most extensive opportunities for profound giving exist. The male-female polarity is thus essential to expressing the kindness characteristic of God in Whose image we were created. This is yet another reason Judaism does not smooth over the differences between the sexes in an attempt to "equalize" everyone.

An article in *Newsweek* entitled "Guns and Dolls" bore the following blurb: "Alas, our children don't exemplify equality any more than we did. Is biology to blame? Scientists say maybe — but parents can do better, too."

This view is anathema to the Jewish position, which tries to foster further development along those lines of uniqueness that already exist. The parents of an artistic child may desire that he or she learn how to play piano in order to be "well rounded," but they will spend much more money on art lessons to develop the child's natural gifts and thus maximize the God-given potential. They will do so because they are not anxious about or threatened by the implications, in terms of human worth, of artistic talent as opposed to musical talent. So, too, should it be with raising boys and girls.

Realistic parents and educators ensure that those qualities and skills most people possess in some measure are developed to an appropriate level in all children. At the same time, great attention is focused on fostering those specific attributes with which the child is gifted by virtue of having been born male or female.

The cornerstone of the entire Jewish view of male and female roles, then, is the premise that gender differences are real and good. They were created with great wisdom and are meant to be acknowledged and used creatively and constructively.

The description of woman's creation in the Torah provides the key to understanding the most encompassing, inherent difference between the sexes. There are many ways in which God could have created the second person who was to be woman. Adam could have been divided into left and right, top and bottom, or front and back. However, God chose to make the division in an entirely different way.

The first person, the Torah tells us, had been formed from *adamah*, earth, a substance truly external to man. When the male-female division was made, it was man who retained both this quality and the name Adam.

Woman is described as being built from Adam's rib, an internal part of the body that protects the vital organs. This gives us a fundamental insight into the nature and role of woman and the consequent interaction meant to take place between the sexes. Woman is to be the internal and spiritually protective "half" of the original whole that was the generic Adam. Woman is thus to be the primary bearer and guardian of internal consciousness for humanity.

Individuality

No person is completely female or male. While each sex is defined primarily by its own attributes, each individual is characterized to some degree by the opposite sex's traits as well. This psychological approach is paralleled by the physiological fact that men and women's bodies produce not only androgen or estrogen respectively, but also a lesser amount of the hormone characteristic of the opposite sex.

In order to develop a clearer understanding of the generalizations that follow, let us draw some parallels from the observable physical differences between the sexes. While women on the whole are smaller, less hairy, and so on than men, there are individual women for whom this is not true. This does not negate the truth of the generalization. Similarly, while universal differences are not subject to change (without surgical intervention), one can sometimes differ from the norm.

Women on the whole do not run as fast as men. The truth of this is so easily observed that there are no serious races in which men and women compete with one another. This is because all women, relative to men, are genetically programmed to develop significantly fewer muscle cells, to have an additional layer of fat, and to distribute and store their fat in a way that is less conducive to moving fast. Even so, a woman athlete, through training and exercise, may lose and/or redistribute fat and strengthen the muscle fiber she has to the point of being able to run more quickly than most men. Nevertheless, the preexisting difference is real; men will run faster than women their age and of the same level of fitness.

This principle applies likewise to psychological differences.

An individual woman may have an inherently more "male" mind than most men, and an individual man's psyche may be inherently more "female" than that of most women. Either may likewise succeed in training some aspect of the mind to think differently from its natural predisposition. Neither of these facts, however, contradict the idea of innate psychological gender differences in the human race as a whole.

Having said all this, be assured that Judaism does recognize the obvious reality of individuality across gender lines. People must honestly acknowledge their identities both in a general and a specific way in order to maximize their contributions. In the particular cases where Jewish law does not permit exceptions to a rule, one must assume one of two possibilities (and one can speculate as to which applies): either the sex difference implicitly underlying the law is seen as being universal, or structuring the law in a way that would consider personal exceptions is impractical. Within the parameters of Jewish law, however, no woman who is a genuine exception, as a result of either God-given or acquired aspects of her personality, should feel compelled to contour herself to a mold at the expense of expressing who she truly is.

A word of caution: Regardless of one's personality and talents, one must take care not to fall into the trap of glorifying the exception without equally affirming the norm. At the heart of this book lies the belief in uncompromisingly endorsing what God has given each of us, and by definition more of us are common than uncommon. The popular bias toward achieving individuality through being an exception stems from a superficial appraisal of people and their souls and the corresponding inability to perceive true individuality in all its subtle beauty. If one would truly get to know any spiritually aware person, no matter how "typical" he or she may appear, one would discover worlds of variation.

God made every human being unique, and each of us must acknowledge our own individual selfhood. At the same time, if we believe that God created both men and women for a reason, and if we wish to enhance rather than deny what we have been given, then we should explore deeply those feminine qualities with which women have been blessed and embrace them with gratitude and appreciation.

With this preface in mind, let us turn to the differences between men and women as Judaism sees them.

Observable Physical Differences

The universal differences, which are most significant to our discussion, are those that exist across the board and unequivocally define one as being either male or female. The most obvious difference is in the reproductive systems – men's reproductive organs are largely external; women's are internal. Each gender's experience of sexuality in its broader sense follows these same lines. A man's most direct experience of his masculinity comes primarily through the external act of sexual relations. A woman, whether or not she has an ongoing sexual relationship, constantly experiences her femininity through the internal processes of menstruation and/or pregnancy, childbirth, and lactation.

Judaism views all physical reality as a reflection of a deeper spiritual reality. In reference to humans, this means that God created our bodies to express our souls. In Genesis, God says to the angels, "Let us make the human in our image, after our likeness." Rashi, the foremost biblical commentator, explains "after our likeness" as referring to those spiritual-intellectual qualities of comprehension and discernment given to humans that make them similar to God. "In our image" Rashi explains as "in our imprint," meaning that we are in a sense a physical portrait of our Creator.

How can this be, given that God Himself has no physical form? Being "in His imprint" means that we reflect something of God in our external selves. Our bodies therefore mirror the Godliness contained within our own souls. The body is the soul's vehicle of self-expression. Each limb and organ of the body parallels an aspect of the soul and has a function that is not only physical but also spiritual.

In rabbinic literature, the commandments, which are the means for the soul-body entity to best express itself, are likened to the limbs and organs of the human body. Accordingly, the various distinctions between men and women in the precepts intended for each are of deep spiritual significance.

It follows, then, that those differences between the sexes that we observe in the physical realm — generally characterized as external (male) versus internal (female) — are paralleled by related differences in the intellectual, emotional, and spiritual realms.

Intellectual Differences

God is understood as having ten primary attributes called "*sefirot*," or emanations. Seven of these are emotive, and three are cognitive. In most systems of delineating these attributes, the three cognitive emanations, which comprise a triad, are referred to as *chochmah* (wisdom), *binah* (insight), and *da'at* (analysis of thought).

Insight and analysis are the two qualities upon which we must focus our attention. Insight means understanding one thing from the midst of another. Analysis means the ability to analyze the external relationship of one thing to another. Insight tends to be holistic and focuses on broad concepts; analysis is particularistic.

While both men and women may have brilliant minds, their thought processes are not identical. Judaic sources state that in order to make mutual contribution possible, God made most men stronger in analysis (thus the area of their main contribution) and most women stronger in insight.

Before giving the Torah, God addressed Moses: "Say this to the house of Jacob and tell it to the children of Israel." Our Sages note that "house of Jacob" is a reference to the women and that the women received the Torah first. Since the Torah was not given twice, this means that the women truly "heard" – received and integrated – the Torah before the men were able to equally integrate the information.

When looking at the contemporary phenomenon of Jews from nonreligious homes choosing to become religiously observant, one notices a difference between the men and their female counterparts. Women usually question the meaning of Torah and its way of life. Men generally are more focused on the structure of Torah and its way of life. The result of this difference in approach is that after a year or so many young women have reached a very complete level of personal integration of Torah, while in the same amount of time their male counterparts are still very "fresh." A few years down the line they will have come to the same place. The women's initial edge will become less significant, and the men, with their analytical approach, will be equally integrated.

Needless to say, everyone uses both insight and analysis. If a man and a woman in San Francisco see someone jump off the Golden Gate Bridge, for example, no man would be so purely analytical as to say, "Hmm...how many miles per hour is he falling?" Nor would any woman be so solely insight-oriented as to think, "Gosh, what could have brought him to this desperate act?" so that she would be surprised when he hit the pavement. Still, each sex favors a different intellectual proclivity.

Insight and analysis clearly serve different interests; in some situations one will be of great benefit and the other will be less so or even a liability, while in other cases the reverse will be true. The potential pitfall of insight is inaccuracy and/or superficiality; the potential pitfall of analysis is never seeing the forest for the trees. It should therefore be clear to any reasonable person that neither quality is inherently superior to the other. However, since insight and understanding are less marketable than analysis, it has become fashionable to disinherit insight with a wave of the hand and a return-to-sender mentality. This can only lead to both personal and societal self-destruction.

Emotional Differences

Men and women share the entire spectrum of emotions; both experience love, hate, hurt. Women tend, however, to be more emotionally responsive and self-aware, more often in touch with their own inner selves. This is due in large measure to the direct connection between the intellect and the emotions, because emotions occur in response to what the intellect perceives. If information is perceived through different means, that is, through insight rather than analysis, the result will be a different emotional response. A woman's deeper sensitivity to what is really happening will awaken in her correspondingly greater responses in the world of feeling.

Other Significant Psychological and Behavioral Differences

The Torah notes that the first woman was created to be with man — woman was created in the context of a human relationship. She was later given the name Chavah, reflecting her status as the *eim kol chai*, the "mother of all living creatures." (*Chavah* and *chai* are derived from the same root words in Hebrew.) Women's heightened consciousness of the value of human relationships predisposes them to spiritual nurture. Women, more than men, focus on the inner lives of the people with whom they interact. This aspect of women has been commented on by various feminist writers and psychologists (most of whom, in contrast to Judaism, do not attribute it to anything inborn).

Dr. Jean Baker Miller, in *Toward a New Psychology of Women*, has described women as "active participants in the development of others." Both she and Carol Gilligan, author of the acclaimed *In a Different Voice*, have noted that women perceive their very sense of self as inseparable from interpersonal relationships.

Connected, perhaps, to these nurturing, relationship-oriented propensities is the fact noted in traditional Jewish sources that the female libido is less likely to operate in the absence of accompanying positive emotional factors; women are less capable than men of externalizing their relationships.

Judaism further recognizes that women are less prone to physical aggression. These particular realities are well acknowledged sociologically and admitted to (albeit grudgingly) by even the most adamant believers in essential male-female sameness. They are evidenced by, among other things, the fact that sexual offenses and violent crime are rarely committed by women.

Spiritual Differences

Spiritual reality (God's Presence in the world) is also perceived in different ways. Most men develop spiritual consciousness primarily through *emet* (truth), the ability to perceive reality in its external manifestation (i.e., the way God has created truth to appear to us in this world). Truth, in human terms (for in its purest sense truth belongs only to God), is generated by a search for information that will bind together and encompass as many aspects of reality as the human mind can grasp. This information is gathered by searching outside oneself (by studying Torah, observing the world, etc.).

Most women's primary source of spiritual consciousness is *emunah*, commonly translated as "faith," but more precisely defined as trust in and complete attachment to God. This trust has its origin in the intense vision of God as a force that rules and is faithful, a vision that transcends the apparent reality of this world. Trust comes not from the outside world but from deep inside one's soul.

As with insight, trust is good only to the extent that it is used appropriately and in the right circumstances. There is a time and place for an appraisal based on obvious truth; faith alone can be dangerous if misapplied. But when focused correctly, trust is a powerful force.

How trust ideally operates is seen in several instances in Jewish history. Preparatory to entering the Land of Israel, for example, Moses sent forth spies to assess the military strength of the Canaanites, who then occupied the land. Ten of the twelve spies returned with a terrifying report, concluding that the children of Israel would never be able to prevail against the Canaanites. The Israelite men in this instance, following the dictates of observable truth, were ready to turn back.

The women, however, guided by trust, would not believe that the land that God had promised them could be unconquerable, no matter how it might appear. Their vision of His power, which had been demonstrated when He took them out of Egypt and performed many other miracles for them preceding and following their redemption, did not allow them to despair. Rather, they maintained their belief that they would succeed and settle in the Land of Israel.

The Jewish understanding of trust is very different from the faith that characterizes other systems of religious thought. Trust here means retaining an image of the way things should be, not the way the believer would like them to be. The entire notion of a "leap of faith" is likewise very foreign to Judaism. Leaping implies moving from where one is to a place beyond. Trust in the Jewish sense implies maintaining with constancy the sense of attachment that is already real.

Hence the Torah says that during the battle between the Jewish people and their enemy Amalek in the desert, Moses' hands were "*emunah*" (conventionally translated as "steady"). The

Amalekites attacked the Jews for one reason only: to break their sense that spirituality is the controlling force in the world. Moses' response was to retain the already existent faith that was part of himself and the Jewish people as a whole. Therefore, the earliest Aramaic translation of the Torah renders the phrase "his hands were *emunah*" as "his hands were extended in prayer."

The inner vision of spiritual reality that trust entails inspires a woman to bring holiness not only to herself but to her husband and children and everyone around her. Throughout the ages women have succeeded in conveying this sense of attachment and faith with great sacrifice and success.

In Conclusion: Feminine Spiritual Self-Expression

We are all multifaceted. Sometimes revealing one part of ourselves requires a repression of other parts. Historically, outside the religious world, women's expression of what is specifically feminine has led them to repress what is general and human. More recently, the discovery of what is general and human has led to the repression of what is specifically feminine. The Jewish view has always been to aim for a realizable picture of self, which includes totality of expression and totality of self-discovery.

Three

Power: Public and Private

The feminist movement stemmed from women feeling disempowered. Men clearly controlled (and still control) the reins of power in the political, financial, and judicial spheres, which determine most of the obvious facets of personal and societal existence. Thus, a primary goal of the women's movement has been to demand a share in this power through equal pay and equal employment opportunities.

Power, in essence, is the ability to effect change. If women have financial clout or high political or business positions, it is thought, then they, too, can determine the changes that will affect their lives and the lives of others.

But the feminist crusade has failed to recognize another, more subtle, form of power: internal power, the ability to affect other people's ethics and values. While external power may procure a high corporate position, internal power will determine whether that corporate executive will be honest or embezzle from the corporation.

Women's quest for external power has left a frightening vacuum in Western society in the area of moral training, where women formerly held sway. Rampant crime, child abuse, kidnapping, and violence against women are symptoms of a society gone amok, where many people have no concept of right and wrong, of honesty, fairness, compassion, or self-control. Only a generation ago, American stores did not have security devices or guards checking bags at every exit; the prevalent sense of honesty made shoplifting a rare occurrence. Such basic morality now seems as outdated as propeller planes.

Today's internal decadence is eroding the quality of life in America as fast as external political and technological advances are improving it. Violence against women has risen dramatically in America in the last decade. After the 1999 Woodstock concert ended in flames, reports began to come in that women there had been assaulted. The official response, says NOW NYC President Galen Sherwin, was to deny that the assaults occurred and to dismiss their importance.

A report published in *American College Health* (September 1997) uncovered a shocking statistic. One out of fifteen young women surveyed reported they had been forced to have sexual relations. Clearly, the lot of women cannot be improved by political and financial progress if the inner dimension of society — its morals and compassion — is neglected by the very people who have traditionally been its custodians: women.

A typical male analysis of such societal problems customarily blames them on external factors; for example, low-income families with many children in impoverished neighborhoods inevitably leads to a high rate of violent crime and substance abuse.

If this were true, then Jerusalem's religious neighborhood of Meah Shearim, which has one of the highest poverty rates in Israel and where families typically number seven to ten children in a three-room apartment, should be a hotbed of violent crime. Instead, Meah Shearim has virtually no violent crime and very little substance abuse despite the total absence of policemen on its streets.

A materialistic society that recognizes only that which can be counted and measured (income, titles, degrees) is bound to discount the imponderables such as compassion, courage, and selflessness, which ultimately determine the fiber of its citizens. Almost none of the heroic gentiles who risked their lives to hide Jews during the Holocaust were people of stature, wealth, or academic achievement. Most of them were simple people whose mothers had imbued them with lofty morality. Typical answers to the question "Why did you risk your life and the lives of your family to hide Jews?" were "My mother taught me to help people who are suffering," or "My parents taught me that no one should be persecuted because of his religion."

Ultimately, the people who had the most significant effect on who you are today were not the president of the United States and the CEO of Bank of America, but your parents, teachers, and childhood role models — the people who influenced your internal development. The wielding of internal power, while rarely accompanied by impressive titles or salaries, has a deeper, longer-lasting effect than the external power maneuvers of those who dominate the nightly news.

Women are the most proficient wielders of internal power because of their preponderance of insight, the intellectual vehicle of entering the very heart, mind, and soul of another person. Insight accounts for mothers usually being able to understand the differences in their children more readily than fathers; for women historically being the pioneers in establishing orphanages, mental hospitals, and homes for the retarded; and for the no doubt accurate feminist claim that if women ran the world there would be fewer wars. The ability to view events in terms of their human cost rather than their political ramifications derives from insight.

The Bible is full of accounts of great women whose exercise of internal power had decisive effects on Jewish history. Sarah understood the negative moral impact of Ishmael's effect on Isaac. She insisted that he be sent out of the household. Abraham could not bring himself to do it until God emphatically told him, "In all that Sarah says to you, hearken to her voice." Commentators on this verse state that Sarah was a greater prophet than Abraham – she could see the long-range moral corruption that could jeopardize future generations of the Jewish people through exposure to a violent and ruthless example at a formative stage.

Rebecca also clearly intuited the inner makeup of her twin sons, Jacob and Esau, and took a decisive, even deceptive, step to ensure that her husband's blessing would go to the son more suitable to carry the mantle of the patriarchs.

The Sages of the Talmud (that portion of Jewish law that was originally oral but is now written) credited the redemption from Egypt to the merit of the righteous women, who, against the judgment of their husbands, saw that they must continue to procreate despite Pharaoh's death sentence on all Jewish male babies.

In all these delicate situations, the women's ability to perceive the reality of a person or situation determined the course of Jewish history.

Thus, defined Judaically, the issue is not whether women should or should not have power, but rather on what kind of power they should concentrate, both for their individual development and for the good of the whole society. This choice is almost totally hidden from women in secular society. Little wonder that those who aspire to grow in an externally directed culture should define their success in terms of external roles and quantifiable achievements. The challenge of excelling in an inner domain is not only unrewarded by contemporary society, but is virtually unrecognized as a possible pursuit. It is not just that the inner race offers no prize money; it is not even listed in the daily double.

Women as Rabbis

Let us examine the issue of women becoming rabbis from this perspective. A student of mine from a Conservative Jewish background told me that as a teenager she had exhibited very spiritual tendencies. She loved to spend time in the synagogue, attended every possible service, and prayed with deep devotion. Her father, among others, used to tell her, "You should become a rabbi."

Now this was years before any branch of Judaism even discussed ordaining women, but people could relate to her inner longings only by slapping an external role and a caption on them. No one ever suggested that she channel her spiritual tendencies into pursuing greater love of God, higher levels of prayer, or the active self-discipline and selflessness that leads to personal sanctity. Such inner achievements, in which she would have found much happiness and self-fulfillment (which she subsequently pursued in an Eastern milieu), were as invisible in her society as the lost continent of Atlantis and much less interesting. It is reasonable to question, therefore, how many women who want to become rabbis are really just seeking the one outlet they know for their genuine religiosity!

The classic role of rabbi is actually that of a judge, called upon to make legal decisions — rulings according to the Torah and Talmud — in areas that in secular society would be handled by a secular court, such as criminal charges and property disputes. (Two-thirds of the Talmud is, in fact, business law.) In addition, any case involving the far-reaching religious laws of the Torah would also be brought before a rabbi or a *beit din* (court of three rabbis). Even today, when secular courts in Israel and abroad exercise jurisdiction in criminal and civil cases, religious Jews are enjoined by the Torah to refer their disputes to a rabbinical court whenever possible.

Judgment in Judaism is idealized as being completely objective and detached. This is not to say that a judge cannot exercise compassion or take into consideration factors particular to an individual when deciding a case. But that he may do so is only because Jewish law itself encompasses these possibilities. In such situations no less than in any other, only objective criteria are employed.

Women use their insight to enable them to see the world through someone else's eyes and thus to identify with and deeply understand the other person. This kind of involvement and connection is the antithesis of the function of the judge.

Carol Gilligan, noted researcher on female development, believes this alternative understanding of justice to be part of the "different voice" that more often characterizes women. Males, she observes, typically conceive of justice in terms of competing rights, a view that requires a mode of thinking that is formal and abstract. Females are more likely to be concerned with conflicting responsibilities that people are seen to have toward one another. Women, therefore, in grappling with questions of justice, tend to think more along contextual and narrative lines. In Jewish terms, this "second voice" is sourced in insight and in a worldview that places human relationships at the center, both of which are part of women's unique endowment.

In short, Judaism does not maintain that women *cannot* develop pure objectivity and suppress their insight so that they can mete out justice fairly, but rather that women *should not* direct their faculties in a way that would be destructive to them as individuals and to the world. Just as society needs judges who can objectively punish criminals and protect innocent property owners, it needs people (counselors, social workers) who can work toward changing the person whose life has brought him to such destructive behavior.

Unfortunately, in our society a judge gets a title, a robe, and a $50,000 salary, while a social worker gets an impossible caseload and a subsistence wage, leading everyone to believe that the judge is more important. We need to honestly consider who is making the greater contribution: the judge who sentences Jack to life imprisonment for murder or the counselor who can help Jack resolve his anger and resentment so that the crime is never committed?

Women as Witnesses

For much the same reason that women are disqualified as judges (i.e., rabbis), they are also disqualified as formal witnesses in court cases. The Torah makes witnessed testimony subject to many technical requirements before it can be used to convict. For example, there must be two witnesses. They must have seen one another at the same time as seeing the crime. If a third person who is technically unqualified simultaneously witnessed the act, the testimony of the first two witnesses is invalidated.

In terms of the individual, he or she may be disqualified from testifying for different reasons. There is a category of people who are disqualified because the accuracy of their testimony cannot be trusted (such as a young child or an insane person). Other individuals are disqualified not because they lack credibility, but because factors such as relationship or societal position render them technically inappropriate as witnesses (relatives of the plaintiff or defendant, kings, the Messiah). *Tosafot*, a leading Talmudic commentary, specifically puts women in this latter category. Since they do not generally divorce the accused's actions from who he is as a person, they are put in the same classification as relatives.

That a woman is disqualified as a witness does not mean that her testimony is never accepted in court. In legal matters in which only credibility, as opposed to witnessing, is required (such as taking an oath that one did not misuse a borrowed object or identifying a corpse), a woman's testimony is accepted. Even in cases requiring witnesses, if technically acceptable witnesses are not available, credibility is deemed sufficient and a woman's testimony is accepted. In such instances, if the judge feels he knows where the truth lies as a result of the evidence before him, he may go ahead and decide the case. All contemporary rabbinical courts follow this practice. It is only in cases where the judge does not know where the truth lies that he must convict a person based only upon testimony supplied by technically acceptable witnesses. Thus Jewish law differentiates between credibility and technical power to convict.

To put most women in the role of technical witnesses is to force them to suppress the wholistic perspective with which they naturally perceive the world. A Jewish court, which idealizes complete objectivity, focuses on two questions: whether a certain action was committed and, if so, whether it was deliberate or accidental — not whether it was justified according to the circumstances.

Imagine a case where you know that a stepfather has been physically and emotionally abusing his stepson from the time he was a young boy. When the boy is eighteen, in the midst of yet another humiliating encounter, he pulls out a gun and shoots his stepfather in your presence. You are a woman who is called as a witness against the boy, and you are asked, "Did you see the accused aim a gun at his stepfather and pull the trigger?" The only answers acceptable to the court are "yes" or "no." As a woman (whose natural tendency would be to answer, "Yes, but..."), would you not feel forced into an untenable situation, where, by abstracting one (albeit fatal) detail of the event you are made to deny the total picture that you perceive?

Judaism seeks to eliminate such victimizing of the witness, so it does not give women that function, just as it does not permit women to be executioners, another role contrary to their true nature. Interestingly, in many of the crimes for which the Torah stipulates the death penalty, the witnesses who testified against the accused must be the ones to execute him. A direct connection thus exists between sparing women from being executioners and sparing them from being witnesses.

External and Internal Domains

It is true that in many communities today where Jews do not concern themselves with what is or is not permitted by the Torah, the rabbi does not function as a judge at all. Such Jews do not call their rabbi to ask if they can eat a meat stew that they accidentally stirred with a dairy spoon, or if during the year of mourning following a parent's death they are permitted to attend a fundraising dinner with background music, or if it is a violation of the laws prohibiting "evil speech" to tell people that they got a divorce because their spouse had a violent temper (all typical questions an Orthodox rabbi is routinely asked).

In such communities, the term *rabbi* has come to denote social director, family counselor, teacher, sermon-giver, and leader of communal prayer. Women in the religious community have always had access to the first three functions without the title of rabbi. Why women are not assigned the latter two demands an understanding, not of the issue of judgment, but of public versus private roles.

The laws and practices of Judaism are a master plan for personal and societal transformation. They reflect the polarities of the internal and external differences between men and women both as statements of the essential nature of each gender and as ideal modes for their respective development. Just as tropical vegetation cannot thrive in the same environment as alpine flora, so too men and women have distinctive general spheres as the settings for their spiritual growth. Thus, the ideal "growing conditions" for most men are in the public domain, while most women can achieve their greatest growth in the private sphere.

Before discussing the particular applications of this principle, we have to take a clear look at both the secular and Jewish concepts of the home.

In secular, male-defined society, the home is a place of confinement and constriction (as it is, in fact, for most men). A person can "go out," that is, have a good time or a broadening experience, or be "stuck" at home. Home is a place in which to sleep, eat, keep one's possessions, and spend time when one has nothing better to do. Even the enjoyments that are available there are poor substitutes for the percieved "real" experiences available outside.

Thus, someone who enjoys listening to records would certainly prefer a live symphony at Philharmonic Hall. Most people who love to cuddle up with a book would find a live lecture by the author more exciting. No wonder that contemporary women have rebelled against roles that confine them to such a limited theater of activity – like aspiring actresses being consigned to eternal summer stock.

In traditional Jewish life, the home serves an entirely different function. The home is the primary place for the enactment of God's commandments.

The primacy of the home in Judaism is apparent in the predicament of American Jewish education during the last few decades. When assimilation and intermarriage became recognized as threats to Jewish survival, the antidote offered by almost all Jewish institutions was "education." The massive effort to give Jewish children a better Jewish education, however, ran up against an indomitable obstacle, which gave rise to a bitter joke.

A knowledgeable Jewish woman was hired to teach in an afternoon Hebrew school. In a short time, parents complained to the principal, "She's teaching our children about the dietary laws, but we don't keep kosher. It's confusing them." So the principal told the teacher to skip the dietary laws. A couple of weeks later the parents showed up again. "She's teaching our children about the Shabbat, but we watch television on Friday night and go shopping on Saturday afternoons. Is she trying to embarrass us?" The principal told the teacher to skip the Shabbat. A few days later, the parents again came clamoring. "She's teaching our children about holiday observances. Do you really expect us to build a *sukkah* (booth) in our backyards and change our dishes for Passover?" Told to skip the holidays, the teacher threw up her hands in frustration. "What," she asked, "do you want me to teach?" "Why," replied the indignant principal, "teach Judaism, of course!"

The crisis of American Judaism is the failure to transmit that twentieth-century oxymoron: Judaism without the home, a hopeless creature that has little chance of survival and virtually no chance to reproduce. Paralleling the devaluation of the home in secular society, certain strains of Judaism have endeavored to replace the home with the synagogue as the central locale for the observance of Judaism. Naturally, therefore, women who want to fully partake of Jewish observance have set their sights on practices that take place in the public setting of the synagogue, such as praying together as a *minyan* (quorum of ten men) and being called to the Torah, while virtually ignoring the practices that take place in the home.

The majority of the Jewish feminist movement's demands for equality thus have as their source the mistaken premise that the synagogue is the most significant place in Judaism and that therefore its roles and functions are of primary importance in Jewish life. The truth is that since the destruction of the Temple two thousand years ago, the home has been and continues to be the holiest and most important place for the practice of Judaism.

And the home is the domain of the woman. This is not only a Jewish concept, but a deep psychological axiom. Among the most basic symbols recognized in psychoanalysis are the enclosed structure symbolizing woman and the soaring tower symbolizing man. These symbols are representative of basic psychological constructs that appear in dreams, drawings, and so on. Traditional Judaism maintains that the woman is the home.

Only in this context can we understand why Judaism assigns women roles that are enacted in the private sphere of the home and assigns men those that take place in the public sphere of the synagogue. Now we can consider, one by one, the various public functions that have become issues for Jewish feminists.

"Why Can't a Woman...?"

We have observed that in many communities today the role of rabbi is less that of a judge and more that of a counselor, teacher, and social director, all areas in which Jewish women have traditionally served. Leading communal prayer, however, is one aspect of the rabbi's role that, in traditional Judaism, is not open to women. Women are not obligated in communal prayer, and only someone who is obligated in a particular commandment can lead others in its performance.

In a broader, more philosophical light, that women do not serve as congregational leaders can be seen as stemming directly from the Jewish understanding that men are the primary bearers of external consciousness in the human scheme. It is men, therefore, who are given public roles in the religious sphere – in order that they may give spiritual expression to this aspect of their maleness. Such roles run counter to a woman's own spiritual development, since her greatest growth will occur through participating in those areas of life that foster the development of an internal perspective on life.

The matriarch Sarah's life provides a profound illustration of this principle. In spending most of her time within the relative privacy of her tent, she reached a higher level of prophecy than did her husband, Abraham.

One who lacks a Jewish understanding of prayer may leave the synagogue feeling that the congregation leader's prayers are somehow more "important," being heard over the voices of the rest of the congregation. The most essential Jewish invocation, the *Amidah*, or *Shemoneh Esrei* (the standing prayer of originally eighteen, now nineteen, blessings) – which is the climax of the entire service – is uttered silently. While one's lips move, the voice is to be audible only to oneself. That this constitutes the ideal form of prayer is learned from a woman – Hannah of the book of Samuel, when she prayed to God that she might have a child. Clearly, then, there is no direct connection between the importance of a prayer and its audibility over a microphone.

Historically, women have led other women in prayer (as they do today in many religious girls' schools) in order to assist those who need help in following the service. This, however, never constituted "leading a prayer service" in the sense of collective articulation, as some women may maintain.

The same understanding of public versus private spheres of expression will explain why women have traditionally not served as presidents of congregations and in other public leadership positions. There is no law prohibiting a woman from serving as a board or committee member alongside men. Many of the more traditional communities nonetheless incorporate a relatively high degree of separation of the sexes in their social and communal involvements, believing that free mingling of men and women can lead, as recent history has proved, to mutual attraction, thus wreaking havoc on the family. Consequently, women in these communities generally do not hold public roles in religious organizations in which both men and women serve.

There is a difference, however, between holding an important public office and doing important work. Many of the jobs done by the organizational leadership in today's communities, such as raising funds, supporting needy causes, and administrating educational projects, are traditionally done by both women and men — without titles.

In my teens I knew a woman who was a hidden pillar of her community. She ran a storefront used-clothing bazaar that provided the poor with clothing and the *yeshivah* (Jewish school) with funds. I saw her again recently, twenty-five years later, zealously collecting for some charity. She, and others like her throughout the ages, neither endeavored nor wanted to receive formal positions of leadership, yet who could dispute the importance of her contribution?

Sometimes, of course, the needs of the community require involvement beyond the personal level. Hundreds of religious women have founded and run organizations to help the poor and the handicapped. The names of these women usually do not appear on fancy letterheads, and dinners for public tribute are not generally given in their honor (things that men, more than women, seem to find important). In fact, these women tend to shun personal publicity and recognition. Nevertheless, their work is not thought of as any less important than that which is done by people who bear titles such as "president" or "executive director." The impact of these women on the lives of others is enormous, which is, after all, what counts most in public service.

The issue of women not being counted for the *minyan* of ten men necessary to say certain prayers is probably one of the most sensitive issues on the agenda of Jewish feminists, because it makes many women feel that they do not count as human beings. This is certainly not the Torah's intention. Rather, the Torah's concept of counting can be understood from looking at the end of the book of Genesis, where we find the number of Jews who descended to Egypt. The text reports seventy "souls" and proceeds to name seventy men. Yet we know that many women also went down to Egypt. The resolution of this discrepancy is found in the beginning of the book of Exodus, where in a similar recounting the text uses the phrase "a man and his household" — that is, each man counted included his family.

The underlying idea is that a woman and a man together constitute one soul. He is the external force, the one who is counted communally, and she is the internal force. (We must remember that until the modern era virtually all women were married. When either a man or woman is single, the picture becomes more complex. There is frustration and loneliness, both of which on the deepest level stem from spiritual incompletion.) This is not just a sentimental idea, but has real legal ramifications. Thus, in the commandment of lighting the Chanukah candles, which a woman is obligated to perform, the husband lights for both of them. Similarly, if the husband cannot light at the proper time, the wife's lighting counts for both of them.

Men are counted in a *minyan* for the same reason that they are the ones who lead communal prayer services: their mode of self-expression is more external. This external drive must be channeled toward development in the highest form, service of God. Therefore, public prayer, proclaiming God's greatness, is an appropriate vehicle for male, outward-bound energy. Seeking to masculinize women by "counting" them as the bearers of external, communal consciousness denies the legitimacy of their role as the inner voice.

When people talk about egalitarianism in Judaism, invariably they mean giving women roles that are traditionally masculine. They rarely, if ever, talk about giving men roles that are traditionally feminine. Do those who would advocate an "egalitarian quorum" similarly demand that men be given equal access to lighting Shabbat candles? That married men be required to cover their hair? That the answer is negative reflects the continuing delegitimization of the uniqueness of womanhood and of feminine power. Women who seek "egalitarianism" through masculinizing their own prayer service are as guilty of belittling themselves as were the blacks who endeavored to look more like whites by lightening their skin and straightening their hair.

Part of what is entailed in the external consciousness required for a *minyan* for prayer is sacrificing one's individuality to the collective whole. This is not viewed as desirable or even fully possible for women. The Talmud states that "one hundred women are not a community but one hundred individuals." When women, with their unique inner consciousness, view themselves not as a communal unit but as individuals, their effect on themselves and others is strengthened.

Certain commandments require hearing rather than reciting a text, such as hearing *Kiddush* (the blessing over wine to sanctify the Shabbat) and hearing the Purim story chanted from a valid *megillah* (scroll) on Purim. In these cases, one person recites, and the others present fulfill their obligation by listening. According to the law, a woman is permitted both to make the blessing over wine and to read the *megillah*. Since external roles are essentially masculine, however, if it is at all possible to give a man the opportunity to do what he was created for, that is preferable. In a situation where no man is available, a woman may read the *megillah* or recite the blessing because of her need to hear it. Thus, Judaism differentiates between a person who is living out a role and one who is fulfilling an obligation.

The issue of women receiving *aliyot* (summons to say the blessings before and after the Torah reading in prayer services) also does not involve a legal prohibition, but rather the principle of giving men the public roles, which are their optimum arena for growth. In this particular issue, a little-recognized factor applies. Only a limited number of *aliyot* are given out, generally seven on

Shabbat mornings and three at other Torah readings. Therefore, every such summons that is given to a woman must be taken away from a man.

Just as women have needs and rights, so do men. I know this is a very unpopular idea nowadays. I read an article recently in which the writer observed that while it is considered absolutely unacceptable to portray a woman as a birdbrain on TV nowadays, it is not considered unacceptable to portray a man as one. A man can be shown tripping over his own feet, being unable to cope, and virtually impotent in the face of the all-knowing Mama (who has taken the place of the once all-knowing Papa).

Part of the reason for this phenomenon is backlash. In making amends for social injustices, people often become extremely sensitive to any hint of the past and are even willing to go to the opposite extreme to affirm real change. But with the sexes, something deeper is going on as well. When people who have been denied the legitimacy of their own role finally gain the opportunity to claim it (or what seems to be it), they can lose sight of other people's legitimate roles and other people's sensitivities and dignity.

Judaically we refuse to allow either backlash or apologetics to distort our vision. It is good to be a woman, and her role goes beyond just not being a man. A man's role, on the other hand, is not to just not be a woman. A man should participate in reading the Torah because performing public roles is both his nature and his challenge.

The Talmud states that it is not in "the honor of the community" for women to make the blessings over the Torah. Not being able or allowed to fulfill one's real potential, especially that which is deep and spiritual, is the ultimate lack of *kavod* (honor). In regard to a commandment that either men or women can perform but that is considered more specific to a man's nature and role, if no man present is competent to perform the mitzvah, a woman may do so, but this is a shameful situation for the men, who should be educated enough to do it. Likewise, the community of men who are counted in a quorum should produce enough men who are capable of saying the blessings on the Torah. Something is radically wrong if that is not the case.

How do people feel when they are pushed out of their own roles? How do they respond in the end? Over the last few years, American society has begun to see male backlash in the form of the "men's movement," which has been desperately casting about for a new (forgotten?) masculine selfhood in the face of what men experience as a usurpation of their former identity by women.

I feel strongly that the only reason Jewish men have not responded with a reverse backlash against women who take the Torah blessings and attempt to take over other traditionally masculine roles is that they are still feeling guilty about men's historical oppression of women in secular society. Sometime soon, Jewish men too are likely to start asking, "Who am I and what's in it for me?" In the end, no sex gains by not respecting the other's right to its role.

The historical fact of the strength and assertiveness of Jewish women throughout the ages is proof that Jewish women have not experienced their exclusion from public roles in the synagogue as a lack of real power. All through our history Jewish women have found their power base in the home to be sufficient and gratifying. The prototype of the browbeaten, downtrodden woman, afraid to express her opinion or to voice disagreement with her husband, is virtually unknown. In the Bible, the matriarchs are usually mentioned only when they did disagree with their illustrious husbands, and the Talmud quotes the maidservant of Rabbi Yehudah HaNasi admonishing her master, the greatest sage of his time. This continues on through the seventeenth century (refer to the journal of Glueckel of Hameln, who, while raising twelve children, also managed a far-flung business enterprise) to modern Yiddish literature, where the women of the Jewish shtetls are usually portrayed as Amazonian matriarchs.

Only in a society that does not recognize internal power and devalues the home could the notion of women as powerless arise. The solution is not empowerment, but "inpowerment" — the recognition of the inner power that has always been available to Jewish women.

Four

What You See Is What You Get: The Laws of Modesty

odesty became an anti-virtue in the latter half of the twentieth century. It is now associated with Victorian prudery, psychological repression, and societal restrictiveness. During the '70s and '80s, personal freedom seemed to be directly correlated with how much skin one could uncover.

Judaism challenges such an equation. It maintains that a woman walking down the street dressed in a tank top and shorts has less freedom than a modestly dressed woman. However much the former may wish to be regarded as a serious person, with an intellect, emotional sensitivities, and talents, most men who see her will not see past her physical attractions. There is an inherent absurdity in a woman's desire not to be regarded as a sex object while dressing in a way that calls attention to her physical attributes.

In considering the issue of modest dress, we must first address the idea of normalcy. If it is normal for women to wear sleeveless dresses, how can it be considered immodest? Clearly the definition of what is normal as opposed to what is abnormal is largely societal.

Our sense of normalcy becomes fairly well frozen somewhere between the ages of three and six. Because we ourselves have grown up in a society in which much of the body being uncovered is accepted, we lack the imaginative capacity to question the implications of such a thoroughly integrated standard of "acceptable" or "normal." What we can question is whether the norms of a given society give birth to and reflect a collective unconscious that is closer to or further from our truest ideals. Let us take a critical look at the society that spawned the drift toward greater body exposure.

Beauty is not only viewed as desirable, but it is central to many women's self-image. The amount of words and paper spent on topics such as weight loss, exercise, diet, makeup, and hair in publications aimed at female readers makes a thundering statement about the centrality of appearance in the lives of Western women.

Clearly, for many women self-worth and appearance have become synonymous; "beauty equals worth" is a message women have absorbed from their earliest conditioning. It is not coincidental that Cinderella was pretty while her stepsisters and stepmother were ugly; it is typical of the vision of a society that equates a woman's qualities with her appearance. "Beauty equals success" is a similar message that billboards and ads repeat over and over until the equation is unquestioned. What are the effects?

One pathetic result is that women, far more than men, seek to freeze themselves at twenty-five to thirty years of age. Gray hair, wrinkles, even smile lines, are viewed not only as unattractive but as reflections of the woman's diminishing value as a person. Thus many women experience a dramatic decline in self-esteem as they age.

While men also value their looks, they tend to equate their self-worth more with the external power they wield in society, such as the ability to command a large income. At the same time, men tend to objectify women much more than women do men. Everyone would acknowledge that throughout history men have sexually exploited women much more than the reverse. This derives largely from men's capacity to externalize reality. It is women, therefore, in their desire to retain their power to attract men, who are the primary victims of the tendency toward self-definition based on appearance. In short, when men age, they become dignified; when women age, they become old.

Many years ago I received a message that some relatives had arrived from abroad. They wanted me to visit them and pick up a package my grandmother had sent with them. Of course, the one time they would be in town was the day before Passover, the busiest day of the year for the Jewish homemaker. Getting a babysitter in Jerusalem right before Passover is not difficult — it is impossible. So, having little choice in the matter, I loaded my five small children onto the bus and set off for the Plaza Hotel. To sweeten their moods, I promised a trip to the zoo to all the good children (leaving the fate of noisy, disruptive children to their fertile imaginations).

When we arrived at the hotel, we were told that my relatives had already left for the day. The children (unlike myself) were not upset or disappointed. The hotel fascinated them. My four-year-old son set his gaze on one of the women tourists sitting in the lounge and could not tear himself away. When I asked what he found so interesting, he looked at this violet-haired, blue-eye-lidded, cerise-pant-suited elderly lady and asked me, "Is this the zoo?"

The moral of the story is that the woman who caught my son's eye had, in her pursuit of eternal youthful beauty, lost something precious. She had lost acceptance of being seventy or so to the point of making herself look somewhat grotesque. The tragedy is that she was probably a fine person whose feelings about herself should have been more self-accepting and positive.

What is the source of women's equating value with appearance? On an apparent level, it is the natural result of living in a culture that is basically materialistic and hence gratification-oriented and superficial. The more gratification on a superficial level is part of a society, the more women will be treated — and view themselves — as objects rather than as people. The victims of this objectification are not only those who are older or less attractive, but young women and beautiful women whose sense of self is stunted by never having focused on their inner — intellectual, psychological, and spiritual — potential.

Tzniut: The Principle of Internality

The Judaic response to human nature's tendency toward superficiality is a set of laws that are categorized under the heading of *tzniut*. The actual definition of *tzniut* is the practical commitment not to allow oneself to be moved into superficial or external definitions of self or others. The result of *tzniut* is to make room for an inner, and therefore more total, vision to emerge. (Since the closest, though innaccurate, English definition of *tzniut* is "modesty," a word with negative vibes in much of today's society, we will continue to use the Hebrew term with its positive connotations.)

Tzniut is a consciousness that the Torah demands both men and women to develop, because it is a prerequisite to possessing a spiritual worldview. Men in Jewish religious society have generally taken it upon themselves to uphold a standard of dress that rivals and sometimes even surpasses that of traditional women. Many men avoid wearing short sleeves and wear shorts, if they do at all, only for sports. Chassidic men wear robes and long coats because such garments are less revealing of the body than a shirt and trousers. In biblical times men always wore robes or tunics; modern pants are a relatively new phenomenon in the religious world.

So why is *tzniut* emphasized more for women than for men? The answer is twofold. Primarily, women are acknowledged to be more inherently gifted in *tzniut* and are therefore more strongly encouraged to achieve in this area of spiritual endeavor. There is also the recognition that men's greater propensity to objectify the opposite sex tends to lead to women's suffering from self-definition based on externalities. For both of these reasons, Judaism directs more specific *tzniut* legislation at women.

Knowing that what we wear says something about who we are, we usually choose to project ourselves by wearing clothes and makeup that make a statement we want others to hear. When you walk down the street, you see people wearing all sorts of statements, ranging from student to artsy ethnic, from businesswoman to cover girl. The ramification of wearing a given uniform is that people relate to you in terms of it. If you are wearing "establishment," you will not be comfortably accepted as a peer by a "rebel," nor are you as likely to be approached by a man as you would if you were wearing "free spirit."

Women generally seek to dress and behave in ways that they know men will appreciate, which all too often means focusing on externality. When a woman then incorporates this view into her own self-image, completing the vicious circle, the results can be pathetic. At the least, she may not be able to envision herself wearing shoes whose heels are low enough so that she can actually walk comfortably. At the extreme, this exaggerated emphasis on appearance can translate itself into the eating disorders that have become so prevalent in our "thin-is-everything" society.

We often fail to realize that how we dress influences not only how others view us, but how we view ourselves. People project back to us the image we intentionally or even unintentionally give forth, and we further internalize it. Even without social feedback, our mere consciousness of the uniform we are wearing impacts directly upon our self-image.

The uniform that the Torah requires of women is dignity. That is nonnegotiable. While all other aspects of self-statement can be determined by individual taste, human dignity remains the focus of the dress code in Judaism.

By observing the laws of modesty, a woman is making the most important statement an individual can make: that she is a total person, not just a body. Secular society too often seeks to express only physicality and diminishes the person in the process. Certain non-Jewish religions, on the other hand, advocate spiritual expression through denying the physical altogether.

Judaism strikes a balance in acknowledging the need for both physical and nonphysical self-expression. Sensuality is channeled into the intimate aspects of one's married life, where it is affirmed and encouraged as a means of expressing one's deepest self to the other. It is simultaneously held back from the public eye, where it will inevitably create distortion and superficiality in how one is perceived. Dress such as spaghetti-strap tank tops, short skirts, and low necklines encourage the casual observer to focus on the body and not on the mind or soul of the woman so attired. Publicly projecting oneself in such a way has the severe spiritual consequence of banishing God's Presence. Modest dress, on the other hand, not only prevents men from viewing women as objects, but, more importantly, allows women themselves to internalize a spiritual self-image.

Some women, upon starting to dress in accordance with the Torah's standards, experience a feeling of disempowerment, no longer able to wield influence over men in the way they once could. This is healthy. A woman's sense of self and power should come not from the number of heads she can turn, but rather from the minds and hearts she can turn.

The problem many women experience is not so much with the principle of modesty as with its specific requirements: sleeves to the elbows, skirts below the knee, necklines to the collarbone. This takes us back to our initial premise — in a superficial, externalized, and materialistic society, modesty cannot feel normal because it is not. Growing up in such a society clearly creates emotional discomfort with the laws of *tzniut*. What inevitably results when we accept the values of that society is equally clear and apparent. As women, the choice is ours.

Judaism sees a direct connection between the qualities of hiddenness and Godliness. Time and time again we observe that what is most sacred is least revealed. In the Tabernacle in the desert, and later in the Temple, the holiest vessels were located in the innermost chambers, where they were least accessible to view. In modern synagogues, the Torah scrolls are kept behind a curtain in a special closet. God's own participation in the world expresses this same theme, for God, the Ultimate Reality, is the most hidden element in the universe.

Thus, Judaism covers the body not as a source of shame nor because it views it as Christianity does, as a base and corrupt member of a person's total entity, but because it regards the body as sacred. After all, the vast majority of the Torah's commandments are performed not through thought or feeling, but through the agency of the body.

In the hallowed realm of relations between husband and wife, the body is thus not only permitted, but is required to be uncovered. Part of Judaism's reason for making parts of the body inaccessible to the public eye is so that when these areas are uncovered in the appropriate circumstances, they will be sensed as part of and exclusive to the personal bond between husband and wife.

It is ironic that in today's extremely exposed and permissive society, many married couples report a difficulty in becoming physically interested in each other. Clearly, if less of the body is exposed in public, more of it will be associated with intimacy, and the more power it will have both to be physically arousing and to create feelings of specialness, singularity, and closeness in marital relations.

The outward expression of *tzniut* is not only in dress but also in speech and behavior, manifested by not taking center stage at every possible opportunity. This self-restraint creates a situation where there is, at some point, sufficient self-confidence to not necessarily need the center. When, for example, a woman refrains from being flirtatious or overly social with men in deference to *tzniut*, she will find that she is forced instead to focus inward, helping to mitigate any need she may have to engage in approval-seeking behavior with males.

The Bible states that when the leadership of the Jewish people in Egypt was passed from Aaron to Moses, "Aaron rejoiced." His sense of self was in no way diminished; in fact, he saw his brother's elevation as his own. He was secure in his understanding of his importance to the Jewish nation, and therefore he did not feel threatened when someone else was occupying the limelight. This quality is part of the essence of *tzniut* and one any human being can benefit from acquiring.

Who Wears the Pants?

Jewish law does not generally permit the wearing of pants by women. Since the upper legs are much more clearly delineated than in a skirt, tight pants can be as provocative as uncovered skin. An additional reason Jewish women have historically not worn pants is that until recently they have been considered a male garment, and the Torah forbids either sex to dress in the clothing of the other.

The unisex image seeks to blur or even erase consciousness of our unique differences, whereas the Torah aims to heighten it. Dressing in a manner that says, "We are both just people, not men and women," ignores the reality that men and women have distinct identities. Of course, today there are pants that are distinctly feminine, and if the upper legs are covered by a tunic, many rabbinical opinions would permit their use. In circumstances where the wearing of pants is dictated by practical considerations (such as cold weather), they may be worn under a skirt and need not be specifically feminine. All of the injunctions having to do with modesty pertain, of course, only to situations in which men are present. Women can wear bathing suits on women's beaches, leotards in women's aerobics classes, and so on.

Covering Hair

One of the laws of modesty requires married women to cover their hair in the presence of men outside the family. That hair is viewed as one of the body's most sensual features is clearly observable in hair-care-product ads, where the imagery is much more in line with the sexual and the sensual than the clean and hygienic. When a woman marries, it becomes even more incumbent upon her not to allow herself to be viewed physically by other men, but rather to reserve all sensual aspects of herself for the intimacy of her relationship with her husband. The principle of a married woman not making her hair accessible to all is one of the cornerstones of *tzniut*.

The fact that divorced and widowed women also generally cover their hair reflects a second aspect of this area of *tzniut* — the reality of a woman's own sexual self-awareness. When a woman becomes directly knowledgeable in sexual matters, her self-image is irreversibly altered; she is more fully conscious of herself as a sexual being. Once this has occurred, whether or not she remains in the relationship, covering her hair serves as a personal reminder of the necessity for safeguarding the privacy of this aspect of herself.

Covering one's hair, of course, does not mean having to forfeit dressing stylishly. There is an abundance of attractive and chic berets, hats, and other head coverings on the market, and creative scarf-tying is an art in itself.

The question of whether or not wigs are permitted to be used as hair coverings has been addressed by rabbinical experts over the generations. While there is not unanimous agreement, many modern authorities do permit them.

People often ask if wearing a wig defeats the purpose of covering one's hair. The aim, however, is not to make oneself unattractive, but unattracting. Jewish women should present themselves well, and women in some societies feel more presentable in a wig than in other forms of hair covering. The aim is to desensualize, not to detract from one's appearance altogether. Whatever wigs are, they are not sensual. Unfortunately, since common sense cannot be dictated, some women select wigs which, while permitted by the letter of the law, clearly are not in the spirit of *tzniut*. This practice is not acceptable to many major rabbinical leaders.

Singing

The Torah prohibits women from singing in front of men. Anyone who has spent five minutes in a religious household can observe that this law obviously does not derive from an attitude that women should be kept mute. Rather, it acknowledges a difference in the type of communication that takes place with song as opposed to speech. Speech reveals ideas and thoughts; it is the vessel of the mind. Song is the vessel of the soul; through the singing voice, one's deepest self can be revealed.

Music has always been recognized as being spiritually and emotionally powerful. Those who are particularly in touch with the ability of music to evoke feelings may sing a melody without words over and over to help raise their spirits toward God. Movies use theme songs and background music to create a desired emotional response in the audience. In the same way, when someone sings, something of that person is being conveyed in an emotionally powerful way, causing listeners to sense who that person really is.

Along with its ability to provide a window into the soul, the singing voice is viewed as a source of sensual attraction when fused with the visual image of the person who is singing, whether that image is present at the time or even just in one's mind. This combination of emotional expressiveness and sensuality is extremely magnetic, as witnessed by the tremendous appeal of many popular singers.

Since women tend to be more internally focused than men, their singing voices are generally more capable of revealing their innermost selves. At the same time, men as a group tend to respond sexually to visual and vocal stimuli more strongly than women. Consequently, when a man hears a woman in front of him sing, he is more likely to feel drawn to her both emotionally and physically. The Torah therefore prohibits a man from hearing women other than his wife and other female family members sing and enjoins a woman from singing in front of other men. Self-revelation joined with sensuality belongs not to the realm of casual social interaction, but to binding and intimate relationships.

Who Owns the Problem?

Since the laws of modesty in Judaism derive in large part from men's tendency to view women as sexual objects, women outside the system may resent that the onus falls on women to dress modestly rather than on men to control their physical urges. One might thus be surprised to learn that there are many laws that restrict men in what they can look at and, as a result, in where they can go.

Men are prohibited from looking at women whose bodies are not covered in accordance with Jewish law. Men are not permitted, given any viable alternative, to go to places where they will inevitably see exposed women or hear female singers. Religious men therefore cannot go to the ballet, the opera, or even the typical circus, while religious women are free to enjoy such entertainment. A woman, properly attired, can enjoy herself at the world's most beautiful beaches, while her husband is confined to the hotel room lest he see women in bathing suits.

Even a man's permission to look at a modestly dressed woman is contingent upon his ability to view her with respect. If he experiences difficulty in this, the responsibility rests on him to avert his gaze. The result is that any religious man not living in a generally observant neighborhood finds his freedom of movement much more severely curtailed as a result of "his problem" than does a religious woman. It is clear to anyone familiar with these laws that the responsibility for creating a society in which women are viewed as people is by no means laid entirely on the woman's doorstep.

There are at least three other reasons why women refrain from exposing as much of their bodies as they might like to and dress with dignity despite the fact that it is man's nature that creates the problem.

Starting with the least self-serving and most altruistic of the reasons, it is good to be able to help another by not placing obstacles between him and his spiritual growth. Both men and women were created with certain shortcomings; one of men's is the tendency to view women physically. This is not meant to reduce men to a bunch of raging hormones, but rather to acknowledge a problem that no doubt a spiritually sensitive man would prefer not to have and must work to control.

Part of sharing in the life of a community means transcending one's self-orientation and taking some responsibility for others. Helping someone to develop spiritually is perhaps the greatest form of loving-kindness one caring person can show to another.

Beyond the aspect of kindness, it is in a woman's practical self-interest to dress with dignity and to be part of a society where that is the norm. Any single woman who has traveled, for example, in a Mediterranean country knows how unpleasant life can be when nearly every male she encounters tries to make a pass at her. One of my students, when she was in her twenties and not yet religious, was determined to travel through Italy alone despite numerous warnings from female friends who had been harassed there. She solved the problem by dressing as a nun.

Of course, a woman need not fear that normal men in a religious Jewish community might similarly approach her should she be dressed immodestly, but dressing with dignity undoubtedly helps men to avoid spiritually detrimental thoughts and consequently to develop into finer human beings. A person who lives in a moral and enlightened community is sure to find life more enjoyable and enriching. In helping men to overcome their own weaknesses, women reap the rewards by being part of a society in which men respect them as people.

Finally, there are clear benefits in terms of spiritual self-image that accrue to a woman who dresses with a sense of herself as a person. The internal focus of *tzniut*, so vital to self-development, opens the heart to a certain type of strength and fearlessness that can be acquired only by not being dependent on the outside world for self-definition.

A woman is empowered with the ability to dress and conduct herself in a dignified, truly self-expressive manner and in so doing to subtly command respect. As a result she is freed to experience the fullness of who she is as a person. This is liberation in its most meaningful sense.

Five

The Spiritual Path of Jewish Women

U p to this point, we have focused on what Jewish women do not do. Unfortunately, in the non-Orthodox Jewish world during the last twenty years, consideration of woman's role has been largely in such negative terms: "Why can't a woman do...?" Rarely are symposiums held on what the spiritual life of Jewish women traditionally has consisted of, as if Jewish women for the last three millennia have done nothing except diaper babies while their husbands rose to spiritual heights through prayer and learning.

In fact, no one truly knowledgeable of Jewish history could contend that Judaism throughout the ages has produced more saintly men than saintly women, only that the former have had more publicity. For a religion that maintains that the world is sustained by the merit of thirty-six hidden saints, obviously fame is no measure of spiritual attainment.

Prayer

One of the basic spiritual practices of Jewish women for the last 3,650 years has been prayer. Indeed, the Talmud tells us that because He loves the prayers of the righteous, God deliberately made the matriarchs barren so that they would have to pray for children.

It is of great significance that the laws of prayer were developed by the sages of the Talmud by using a woman, Hannah, as the role model. Her prayers, as narrated in the first chapters of the book of Samuel, contain within them the very core of Jewish prayer structure. Specifically, the following practices stem from her methods:

1. She prayed silently. The central prayer of every Jewish prayer service – the standing prayer of nineteen benedictions – is always recited under one's breath. This signifies that God hears our thoughts and does not need them verbalized. The need to use speech in prayer at all is related to the way we are affected by the sound of our words and by the way they involve us and delineate our thoughts for us. We do not allow ourselves the luxury of being so wrapped up in our own self-expression that we lose our sensitivity to God's transcendence. Hence our prayers are verbal, but in deference to Hannah's insights into prayer's true nature, they are silent.

2. The text explicitly makes note of Hannah's prayer as being an outpouring of her heart. Too often prayer is said by rote, the focus on completing the service rather than its genuine essence: prayer as connection between oneself and God.

Although according to many major *poskim* (interpreters of Jewish law) women are obligated to pray the morning and afternoon prayers (men are obligated in these and an additional evening prayer), all rabbinical opinions agree that women are obligated to fulfill the commandment of "service of the heart" by praying every day in some way. The minimal fulfillment of this would be a short prayer of one's own composition that includes praise of God, a request, and thanks.

The historical reality is that Jewish women throughout the ages have undertaken the saying of the book of Psalms as their specific avenue of prayer. These prayers are particularly suited to women's lifestyles because one can interrupt their recitation at the end of every line (when the baby cries, when the pot boils over, when a neighbor needs a sympathetic ear, when your lunch break is cut short). The standard prayer service should not be interrupted except at certain points, and it is forbidden to interrupt the silent standing prayer at all.

To this day, women can be seen fervently reciting psalms at the Western Wall in Jerusalem at every hour of the day and night. The seriousness and power of their prayer is evident even to the casual observer. And in religious communities throughout the world, women will invariably respond to news of a drastic illness or other impending catastrophe by getting together to recite these songs of praise and supplication.

In this age of modern women earnestly seeking to find their spiritual path in Judaism, it is a shame that the ancient and powerful practice of saying psalms goes largely ignored. Its power to work wonders is attested to by the old saying "Don't rely on miracles. Say psalms!"

Rabbi Meir Fund tells the story of his grandmother, Hinda, and her brother, who lived in Europe before World War II. Her brother's spiritual path was to learn Talmud; he was recognized as one of the greatest scholars in Poland. Hinda's spiritual practice, like that of most women in her society, consisted principally of the fervent recitation of psalms.

On the day that Hitler marched into Austria, Hinda, who was in her late forties and had seven children, went to one of the great rabbis in her city of Vienna. She told him that she knew she would soon be leaving this world and in Heaven she would pray that her children be protected in the impending cataclysm. Three months later she died.

Her seven children were scattered all over Europe: Belgium, Rome, Treblinka, Auschwitz. All seven of them survived the Holocaust. They each have stories to tell of their miraculous escapes, which they attribute to their mother's prayers. Rabbi Fund ends the story by asking, "Who can say which was greater, my great-uncle's Talmud or my grandmother's psalms?"

Jewish women most often pray at home for several reasons. The first is that, unlike men, they are not obligated to pray at set times or in a group of ten. This gives women the freedom to pray according to their convenience (although the morning prayer must be said sometime before noon and the afternoon prayer before sunset), in solitude, and at their own pace, which most women find more conducive to concentration and devotion. In fact, the single most common complaint from men in their early stages of becoming religiously observant is the difficulty of keeping up with the quorum while at the same time concentrating on the words they are saying.

Praying at home is also more convenient for mothers of small children, which is why the ladies' sections of Orthodox synagogues are generally occupied by older women and single girls. This, however, should not be misunderstood to mean that younger married women do not pray.

One of my students told me of a pivotal point on her path toward Torah observance. A very spiritual young woman who spent long periods each day in prayer and meditation, she was afraid that the Orthodox lifestyle would leave her no room for her inner life. Then she was invited to Shabbat dinner at the home of a family with thirteen children. During the meal, she asked the mother if she ever prayed and was surprised to hear that she did – twice every day. Seeing her astonishment, the mother added, "That's nothing. I have a cousin who has sixteen children, and she prays, with concentration, three times a day."

Another reason most women prefer to pray privately relates to the holiness of the Jewish home. Praying there both partakes of this sanctity and adds to it.

In times and places where a large proportion of Jewish women did go to synagogue, the women's galleries are grand and spacious. (Witness the magnificent old synagogues of Calcutta and Amsterdam.) In places and periods where they usually did not, the women's sections were correspondingly paid little attention; some old synagogues have none at all.

A common phenomenon today is for newly religious women, or even tourists, to go to synagogues in Jerusalem's Meah Shearim quarter and complain that the women's sections are cramped and claustrophobic, as if the Orthodox are trying to discourage women from coming to pray. In fact, the builders of these synagogues a half-century or a century ago never expected that these women would be coming to visit or even that sociological changes would cause more of their own women to attend services. One of the newest chassidic synagogues in that area, the Boyaner shul, boasts a spacious, airy, and well-lit women's gallery.

Prayer is a serious spiritual practice designed to connect a person to one's Creator. It is not a spectator sport. That some women complain of their lack of a "view" in synagogue, rather than their lack of prayerful concentration or communion with God, reveals a total misconception about why anyone should be there in the first place.

Once we understand that the purpose of prayer is to develop a connection with God, we gain a new perspective on why men and women sit separately in the synagogue. The ideal state for a person to be in when praying is to envision him or herself as part of the community yet simultaneously alone with God. In order to create an environment conducive to this, distractions are limited. Praying outdoors, for example, is not as desirable in Jewish law as praying indoors. In the synagogue, mirrors are forbidden, and pictures are considered a distraction (which is why there is no true synagogue art parallel to the great cathedral art). A Jew is enjoined not to look out of the windows during prayer. If possible, one should pray facing a wall with one's eyes either closed or looking at a prayer book. Lack of visibility of the opposite sex at this time is part of the generalized effort to eliminate distractions.

Many of the single men and women who complain about *mechitzot* (partitions) that block visibility are at times busy surveying the available members of the opposite sex when the partition is more open. All too often, in synagogues that have mixed seating or very low partitions, the ambience of "going to synagogue" is more like a singles' mixer than a spiritual experience. Partitions were set up to help both men and women accomplish what they came to do: develop a connection with God.

Special Mitzvot for Women

Athough women are obligated in most of the commandments of the Torah, three are regarded as specific to them, designed to meet their unique spiritual needs and potentials. These are

1. *hafrashat challah* – separating a small portion of dough while baking bread;

2. *hadlakat neirot* – lighting Shabbat candles; and

3. the laws of *niddah*, also known as *taharat hamishpachah* (family purity) – the laws pertaining to going to the *mikveh* (ritual bath) after menstruation.

The first two may be performed by a man only if no woman is present who is able to do them. That is, while both men and women are obligated to light Shabbat candles and to separate the dough, women are given precedence, much like a man is given precedence in reciting the blessing over wine. The third, family purity, is one which by its nature may be performed only by women.

The source of these *mitzvot* as being specifically feminine in nature is ancient. The Torah narrates that when Isaac married Rebecca, he brought her "into the tent of Sarah, his mother," who had died three years earlier. The Midrash (narrative portion of the Talmud) comments that the three miracles that were present throughout Sarah's lifetime and ceased when she died returned when Rebecca took up residence in her tent.

The three miracles that occurred in Sarah's tent parallel three particular spiritual acts that she performed and that the Torah ordains as women's commandments. Sarah's candles burned from one Shabbat eve to the next in response to her lighting them. The bread she baked remained fresh all week; this blessing resulted from her sanctifying a portion of the dough that was to be baked. The cloud that permanently hovered over her tent represented the *Shechinah* (Divine Presence, God's feminine aspect) in response to Sarah's observance of family purity.

These three precepts also bear a direct relation to Eve's part in humankind's original wrongdoing. The Garden of Eden narrative describes the essential spiritual and psychological state that characterizes every living man and woman.

Both Adam and Eve, representing collective man and womankind, allowed themselves to be blocked by limited perceptions, which led them to err fatally by eating from the Tree of Knowledge of Good and Evil. Both were subsequently given means of rectifying their wrongs corresponding to the separate nature of their mistakes and to their different capacities and destinies. God's "curses" were not designed to punish as much as to provide an alternative, albeit more uncomfortable, path to achieving the good originally destined for humankind that might otherwise have been forfeited.

The three commandments addressed to women parallel both Eve's mistake and the pain entailed in the situation consequently presented to her. They are meant to enlighten us both as to how we can avoid similar misdirection of our energies and how we can come away from the inevitable difficulties we experience as women with greater clarity and, ultimately, happiness.

Let us first examine the commandment of separating the dough. When making bread in the time of the Temple, it was obligatory to separate some dough for the *kohanim* (priests). To understand this, we must grasp the importance of the Temple, where the priestly service was performed.

The Temple was built along the lines of the *Mishkan* (Tabernacle), the place where God's Presence could be most manifest in the desert. After recording, "Let them make for Me a sanctuary that I may dwell in them," the book of Exodus describes in great detail exactly how it was to be built. The detailing is so specific that a large portion of this book is devoted to its physical structure.

Note that the original commandment does not state that God will dwell in "it" — that is, the sanctuary — but that He will dwell in "them," the Jewish people. The Tabernacle was meant to be a microcosm of the universe, a map by which we could determine how to elevate and sanctify ourselves and the world. Hence, not only is it described as a place where God's Presence would dwell, but as a vehicle for allowing this Presence to dwell within us.

This was similarly true for the Temple. Each detail of the Temple's physical structure and its service was significant in symbolizing a specific method of elevation of a given area of life. The Temple had a chamber, called the "*Heichal*," which contained various features representing aspects of the human body: the Ark symbolized the mind; the Candelabra symbolized the heart or spirit; and a special Table, upon which the showbread was placed, symbolized the stomach.

The parts of the chamber in which these objects were located symbolized how hidden or revealed God's Presence is in that particular aspect of life. Thus the areas of maximum light on the east and the south sides of the Temple were where the Ark and the Candelabra were situated, while the area of least light, the north, was the place of the Table. Eating, as well as the earning and spending that makes it possible, often serves to make people more physically conscious and self-centered and less conscious of both the needs of others and one's obligations to God.

By including the Table in the chamber, the Torah is making a statement — that even such essentially physical experiences as eating can open the doors to spiritual consciousness, as long as one sees the sustenance as coming from God and that there is a willingness to view food not only as something to be taken but also as a vehicle of giving.

Therefore there were twelve breads on the Table, corresponding to the twelve tribes, each of whom contributed something to the totality of the Jewish people. The trays holding the breads were stacked one upon the other to symbolize the fact that the act of contribution constitutes the source of all life and sustenance. The giver and the recipient need one another equally in order for them each to be whole. This bread, like Sarah's, stayed fresh from week to week. Its spiritual vitality kept its physical structure from the normally inevitable process of disintegration.

The commandment of separating the dough involves taking ordinary ingredients of physical life — flour and water — and raising one's awareness of their inherent sanctity. In the time of the Temple, the separated dough was given to the priests to sustain them in their roles as officiators of the Temple service and educators of the people.

The Talmud states that in the absence of the Temple one's home is one's temple and one's table is one's altar. A woman in her home has a specific level of access both to refinement of the physical and to use of it in giving to others. A man's work traditionally consists of bringing home the wheat. The woman refines the wheat and makes it into something that, if addressed with the appropriate consciousness, can nourish others, sustaining not only the body but the spirit as well.

The *mitzvah* of separating the dough thus embodies the essential Judaic statement that reality cannot be compartmentalized, but that both spiritual and physical aspects are ultimately rooted in God. The elevation of physical existence and its unification with the spiritual, as achieved through the performance of this commandment, reflects the entire purpose of human existence.

We see in Genesis that Eve misused her ability to define the physical world as a vehicle for Godliness and for life. By offering Adam the fruit of the tree, thus drawing them both away from God, she caused them to ultimately experience mortality. The specific responses God subsequently addressed to Eve were designed, in part, to foster sensitivity in women as to how they could ideally relate to the world of physicality.

"I will greatly increase your anguish and your pregnancy," God said to Eve. "It will be with anguish that you will give birth to children." This curse of anguish accompanying the physical discomforts of pregnancy and childbirth presents a woman with an unparalleled opportunity: to rise above the mere physical experience and recognize it as a means to a greater spiritual end, that end being nothing less than the bringing of new life into the world.

The precept of taking the dough thus corresponds both to the general challenge of relating to the physical as a vehicle for spirituality and to the consequent difficulties specifically in bearing children by increasing consciousness of how one can draw close to God through these same aspects of life.

The commandments of candle lighting and family purity are each similarly intended to help women meet a challenge and to transmute a potential curse. Candle lighting speaks to the power of feminine spiritual nurture and influence. The human soul is called God's candle. A woman has the specific capacity, in her daily involvement with her family, to reach into the depths of the soul and draw forth that which is hidden, thus catalyzing spiritual potential.

Looked at simply, the lighting of candles before Shabbat and holidays ensures that, as darkness falls outside, the house will be a place of light where family members can interact productively in celebrating the special holiness of the day. Similarly, on a deeper level, the woman holds the key to creating true domestic peace, the harmony in which each family member is made aware of his or her unique potential for holiness. This is the reality reflected in the lighting of these candles.

The Shabbat is referred to metaphorically as a bride or a queen. The Hebrew word *kallah* (bride) comes from the same root as the Hebrew word for "completion"; *malkah* (queen) means "rule" or "direct." Both of these feminine images are reflected in the idea that in lighting candles the woman of the home draws her inspiration to both complete and direct her family.

In the Garden of Eden, Eve made the wrong response to the challenge of how to use her powers of nurture and spiritual influence. The curse of the emotional distress that was to accompany child-rearing largely concerns the ultimate lack of control that a mother has over her child. These emotional challenges can lead a woman to realize that nurturing and exercising power over others can be effective only to the degree that her will reflects God's will.

The commandment of candle lighting instills in women the awareness that they possess the power to ignite souls. It also serves as a beacon through troubling times, turning their focus away from their difficulties and toward the ultimate goal of bequeathing spiritual life to their families and bringing God's light into their homes.

The moment of candle lighting is a time when there is a meeting between God and His children, as He reaches out toward us and we reach from within ourselves toward Him. The custom of praying at the time of candle lighting that one's children be enlightened in Torah came about in realization of the special holiness of this moment.

The laws of family purity govern the physical interaction between husband and wife. (Anyone wishing to learn the laws in complete form should consult a book that treats them in detail or preferably to talk with an experienced teacher of this subject. What follows is merely a brief description.)

Menstruation is a somewhat strange biological phenomenon. As pointed out by Rabbi Aryeh Kaplan in *The Waters of Eden*, it would be more efficient for the body to reabsorb the thickened uterine lining than to reject it every month, causing the entire female organism to be affected. Rabbi Kaplan notes that many biologists see this as an "unexplained inefficiency" in the female reproductive system – a curious imperfection.

Judaism considers everything about the body to be a source of information about a deeper human spiritual truth. Even such a simple fact as the tongue being protected by the teeth and the lips is meant to tell us something about how carefully one should guard one's speech.

What information is the menstrual cycle giving? It is telling us that we are vulnerable and not eternal. Like death itself, it informs us that we are imperfect beings. The need for this consciousness of imperfection derives from the collective human psychological state as described in Genesis.

Adam and Eve initially saw everything clearly as true or false, with no confusing shades of gray. When they disobeyed God, their clarity of perception was muddied. They sought to broaden their freedom to make choices by allowing a subjective vision of morality to become part of their very essence. The effect of this "broadening" was the loss of our highest potential: to know reality as it is without the illusions that are now part of the human psyche.

As a means of rectification, we are confronted with a spectrum of phenomena that break through the illusions. The major one is death. A secondary one is menstruation. Like death, menstruation forces us into true contact with life's realities.

The Hebrew word *tumah*, conventionally and incorrectly

translated as "impurity," is used only in terms of the spiritual and has nothing to do with physical uncleanness. The best translation for it would probably be "blockage." The ultimate blockage is death; a body without a soul is blocked from being able to express any aspect of spirituality. Likewise, all who see death in its stark reality realize how limited and blocked they themselves are by their own mortality. At the same time, if one makes the right choices, death can be a profound means of moving one to recognize that, while physical life is fleeting, the spiritual life that underlies it is enduring and essential.

Menstruation occurs only when the conception of a new life has not occurred. By representing the loss of life potential, it is meant to convey the same message: acknowledge your physical frailty even in that area of life, reproduction, which creates your own finite immortality in this world. At the same time, realize that a soul could have been brought into the world and so sensitize yourself to that aspect of life that is truly eternal, the spiritual.

Blocked and unblocked are not synonyms for bad and good. When a righteous person dies, he or she does not cease to be righteous and become evil. That body, however, becomes blocked because it can no longer express the soul. Similarly, a menstruant woman is not evil, nor is it a sin that she has not conceived. Rather, she is experiencing her own body's limitations.

Modern-day America and many primitive cultures share one attitude in common concerning menstruation: that of denial. In primitive societies, menstruant women were often expelled; the message of mortality that their bodies bore was too frightening to assimilate. In American culture, even though all aspects of sexuality are discussed, viewed, and sung about with great explicitness, menstruation is not. Even in advertisements for "feminine hygiene" products, the approach is "Use this and you can utterly forget that you are having your period."

This avoidance would seem to stem from a desire to escape the physical inconveniences entailed in menstruation. Yet it could reflect a subconscious denial resulting from human discomfort, on a very deep level, with our biological imperfection and the inextricable bond of death to life.

The Judaic response to menstruation is to acknowledge our reality. We are no longer in Eden. We are mortal; our bodies are fragile. Our access to eternity is blocked by our physicality. Denials will not help, but being conscious at every moment of what life means on a spiritual level will. The laws for the menstruant woman are a unique means of allowing her to imbue physical experience with spiritual consciousness.

When a woman enters into this state of blockage, she is called a *niddah*, meaning "one who is separated." She and her husband immediately refrain from all sexual and physical contact. This continues for the duration of her menstrual period, considered to be at least five days, and for an additional seven days thereafter. The woman then immerses in a *mikveh*, upon which she returns to a state of ritual purity. She and her husband then resume their sexual relationship. This is the set of laws that, generally speaking, Sarah observed; in the merit of this observance the cloud of the Divine Presence hovered over her tent.

This Presence is the aspect of God that is hidden in the midst of physicality and can be experienced by our connecting to the spiritual through studying Torah and performing its commandments. It is described as God's feminine aspect both because of its hiddenness and because of its qualities of receptivity and nurturing. It receives the energy created by the fulfillment of a commandment and allows it to ignite and give light, much as a mother is conscious of her children's capacities and encourages them to flourish.

The Torah makes reference elsewhere to a cloud representing the Divine Presence. The commentators tell us that Abraham recognized upon which mountain he was to sacrifice his son Isaac by the fact that he and Isaac saw a cloud hovering over it. This cloud was not observed by Abraham's servant Eliezer or by Ishmael, who accompanied Abraham and Isaac on their journey, since this vision was accessible only to those on a very high spiritual level.

God's Presence represents itself as a cloud because clouds are involved in a similar process of receptivity and nurturing. A cloud draws moisture from the ground and then returns it as rain, which brings life and growth to the earth. In the same way, His Presence draws forth the God-awareness that people allow themselves to feel when performing a commandment and returns it to them in the form of still higher awareness and sanctity.

One of the Torah's decrees is to be holy. Holiness in its classical sense means separation, the ability to remove one's consciousness from absorption in physicality. It is thus possible to transcend the mundane and reach a higher level of awareness. This is accomplished by entering into an aspect of life that is by its nature physical (such as eating or engaging in sexual activity) and experiencing Godliness from that place with the same clarity as one would from a place of less physicality (such as praying or learning Torah). Sanctifying oneself in this way creates a dwelling place for the Divine Presence, a place where Godliness can be experienced.

Judaism views sexuality in marriage as an expression of the couple's deeper spiritual bond. In the temporary absence of physical relations, a couple is encouraged to focus on and further develop those aspects of the marriage that underlie and give spiritual life to their sexual relationship. Periodic abstinence from marital relations thus ensures that the spiritual foundation of the marriage constantly becomes richer, deeper, and stronger, making sexual relations an ever more profound experience. While some popular books take the position that for physical intimacy to be more exciting it must be more physical, Judaism maintains that nothing adds as much power to sexual relations as intense emotional and spiritual connection. The laws of family purity promote the spirituality of the sexual experience and sanctify the couple who observes them.

The Midrash relates that Eve used physical desire as a tool in order to persuade Adam to sin. As a result, part of her curse (rectification) was "To your husband shall be your desire, and he shall rule over you." This, say the commentators, refers to the disadvantaged position of the woman in the sexual realm. Biologically it is not she but he who determines whether and when relations will take place. Psychologically most women tend to not want to be the one to actively initiate relations. The difficulties this creates for the woman are multiplied by the fact that her sexual needs, which also encompass a wide spectrum of emotional needs (i.e., assurance of love, desirability, closeness), are often greater than those of the man.

The laws of family purity redress some of the imbalance in

this area by restricting the power of the man to determine when relations will take place, making this largely dependent on the woman's own cycle. The night of immersion, when sexual relations are actually a commandment, for most women coincides with the time of ovulation, when a woman's biological desire is at its height. In addition, in circumscribing the wife's availabilty, these laws help to guarantee that her husband's desire will match hers. It therefore alleviates the frustration she might otherwise suffer from feeling uncomfortable about expressing her feelings.

The laws of family purity thus ensure that sexuality, rather than being the locus of subtle (or not so subtle) power plays and struggle, will be directed toward its highest purpose: expressing genuine and deep caring in the marital relationship. It furthermore makes the profound statement that a woman's sexuality is not subordinate to any man's desires but to the dictates of a higher spiritual reality, which among other things unequivocally affirms the fullness of her sexual needs.

The observance of the three special commandments for women gives them unique access to an appreciation of their sexuality and creative and nurturing potentials, which allows them to hallow and elevate these vital areas of life.

The Offering of Vulnerability

A precept that applied to women only during the time when the Temple stood offered yet another way for women to relate to and elevate their most fundamental experiences. Although both men and women could bring the various required and optional sacrifices in the Temple (such as the thanksgiving, elevation, and sin offerings), women had a special commandment to bring a sacrifice after giving birth. The offering consisted of a sheep for an elevation offering (if she could not afford a sheep, she could substitute a dove) and "a dove or a turtledove for a sin offering" (Leviticus 12:6). What sin did a woman commit in childbirth?

The function of presenting a sacrifice, according to the major commentators, is to draw one closer to God. The Hebrew word for "sacrifice," *korban*, comes from the root meaning "to draw close." When a person offers a sacrifice, she intends to rectify some distancing from God that she has experienced.

Distancing can occur through one's actions (i.e., committing a physical transgression) or even through one's thoughts and feelings. The subsequent drawing close is accomplished by identifying oneself with the animal that one is offering. This takes place through focusing on the part of oneself that is similar to the animal. One then makes the conscious commitment to employ that same aspect of self in strengthening one's relationship with God.

Sins that involve desire, for example, were generally atoned for by the sacrifice of a goat. Those of you who have ever lived on a kibbutz, moshav (collective settlement), or farm know that a goat will get itself into the most tangled predicaments in order to fulfill every passing desire. Goats will try to go through barbed wire in order to get a piece of garbage on the other side.

There is a part of every person that wants to live life on those terms. A profound and potent expression of the inner resolve to take the energy that says, "I want my desires, and I want them now, whatever the cost," and to refine it is the offering of a sacrifice.

A sacrifice as commanded by the Torah required various

steps. One that was common to all sacrifices was the selection of the animal – the person who would be bringing the sacrifice had to actually choose the goat or ram or bull with which he was going to identify. Another step was placing one's hands on the sacrifice in order to create still further bonding.

All sacrifices required two more rituals that will explain, more than anything, the consciousness that the sacrifice was meant to evoke. After the animal was slaughtered, the blood had to be received in holy vessels. The Torah calls the blood of an animal its soul, meaning that the life force of the animal is contained within its blood. (Scientifically the entire endocrine system, which activates many of the body's responses, is located in the blood, and blood is the vehicle by which life itself is transported to every cell of the body.) The idea of this being receivable in holy vessels means that any energy can be pure and good, assuming it finds the proper receptacle. By electing to put the blood in a holy vessel, the offerer of the sacrifice was symbolically committing herself to taking the energy that parallels the nature of the sacrificed animal and finding for it a pure and constructive vehicle of self-expression. The method is not one of negation, but of positive channeling.

The final phase required burning the corpse of the animal, drained of its lifeblood. This symbolized the reality that there are aspects of ourselves that we have to let go and ultimately burn on our own inner altars. While general energies can be sublimated into pure channels, there are specific desires that may have to be given up. No one can pursue every desire relentlessly and still retain one's spiritual integrity.

Unlike the regular sin offering, the bird offering after childbirth was not brought on the basis of having become distanced from God as a result of a physical transgression, but rather from having experienced negative and destructive thoughts. The Talmud states that the physical and emotional distress of a woman in labor could be such that she might swear to never again have relations with her husband and bear more children. She therefore brought a bird offering to rectify the anger at and subsequent distancing from God that she experienced (and that she would no doubt regret once she held her baby in her arms).

Let us look at this idea in depth. Bird offerings were generally offered after one had undergone a period of suffering, since such an experience can distance one from God if not viewed with the desired consciousness. Childbirth has different aspects, the most salient being the indescribable joy experienced upon seeing one's child emerge from one's own body. But that moment is preceded by a protracted period of vulnerability and pain. Furthermore, each birth process follows its own unpredictable course. The woman in labor is keenly aware of being at the mercy of forces beyond her control.

People react differently to being forced to acknowledge their vulnerability. Many people make denials. Likewise, women often use denial in relating to the pain of labor and birth, whether they seek to escape it through drugs or general anesthesia (as was common in the past) or go to the opposite extreme of proclaiming that every woman can control her own birth experience nonmedically as long as she does the correct breathing. Birthing, however, is by its nature a process that is not controllable by even the most trained and adept human beings. The only thing over which we have control is our response to what we are experiencing.

The sacrifice of a bird is always a symbol of acknowledgment that pain and vulnerability do not have to lead only to denials and escapism; they can also lead to closeness and bonding with God if there is an accompanying realization that one must ultimately place oneself in His hands. A bird, one of the most vulnerable of creatures, has the almost miraculous ability to survive by flying upward. From the perspective of the Torah, it is important that a woman transmit this consciousness to herself after having experienced birth.

Being Commanded versus Making Choices

Just as the Torah obligates women in commandments that are geared to develop their spiritual potentials, so men's are aimed at masculine needs. Women are generally exempt from these latter precepts, although they are permitted to perform most of them if they so choose.

Commandments can be divided into the categories of positive and negative. The function of the negative, or prohibitive, injunctions is to prevent a person from making choices that will block his access to his better and more God-like self. The existence of various prohibitions, such as those against murder and theft, benefits not only society as a whole but also the individual who avoids the undesirable spiritual consequences should he violate them. In terms of the negative commandments, Jewish law obligates men and women identically.

All of the commandments from which women are exempt are in the positive category. Designed to draw forth the best aspects of one's self and to create a spiritually more conscious person, they relate to the capacities, strengths, and life experiences of the particular category of people to whom they are addressed. Priests, Levites, and kings, as well as people who find themselves in specific situations such as coming upon an unburied body, all require laws directed to their unique needs.

The positive commandments aimed specifically at men are in the category of those whose performance is bound to a certain time, such as reciting the prayer of Shema at its proper time in the morning or dwelling in a *sukkah* (booth) during the week-long holiday of Sukkot (Tabernacles). Their observance therefore entails a larger degree of regimentation in one's religious life. Judaism acknowledges that since male consciousness and energies are more outwardly directed than those of females, a man requires more externally imposed guidance in order that those energies find growth-producing expression. Positive time-bound commandments allow men to structure their lives in ways that open up avenues of meaning that for them would otherwise remain closed.

Most women are more likely to feel spiritually "at home" when more of their activities fall into the realm of things over which one has freedom to exercise one's own choice. An individual woman, however, may have a genuine spiritual need for self-expression through one or more of the positive time-bound commandments from which she is exempt. A woman is therefore not forbidden to perform the overwhelming majority of them, and such voluntary performance is considered meritorious. When women accept such an optional precept upon themselves universally, it may even acquire the status of being an obligation for all women from that time onward. An example of this is hearing the *shofar* (ram's horn) blown on Rosh HaShanah (Jewish New

Year's) morning, which women as a whole have traditionally taken upon themselves to observe.

The few commandments that are not open to women are those whose performance would entail technical legal problems that have nothing to do with a woman's spiritual capabilities. The freedom to choose which, if any, of the positive time-bound ordinances she will observe permits her to determine how religious self-expression should take place within the framework of her life.

That men are obligated in more precepts than women is the basis for the blessing that a man says every morning thanking God that He did not make him a woman. Because commandments are the vehicle of connection to God, they are viewed as a precious gift and privilege for which we should be grateful. This blessing appears third in a series of three. The first gives thanks that we are not gentiles, since a Jew's spiritual potential dictates that he be obligated in many more commandments than a non-Jew. The second thanks God for not having made us slaves, which in this case means gentile slaves who have been semi-converted to Judaism. The blessings refer in ascending order to the number of commandments in which one is obligated so that we can instill in ourselves the full consciousness of, and gratitude for, that which God has given us.

So why not have the blessings stated in the positive, thanking God for having made one a Jew, a free person, and so on?

Life is full of stress; the price of growth on all levels is having to meet conflict head on. Even if one seeks to escape growth, stress and difficulty are nonetheless part of living. In short, being on this earth is not easy. Whether or not the struggle is worth it can be seen only at life's end, when the person one has developed into is judged. Until that day, thanking God for a mission that has most likely not yet been fulfilled and an opportunity that has not yet been realized is at best irrelevant and at worst arrogant. Stating the blessings in the positive form would therefore be inappropriate.

Having less external structure in her spiritual life creates difficulty for the woman, as freedom always does. There is also the conflict that playing a panoply of roles — wife, mother, working woman, spiritual seeker — invariably creates. A woman's life is certainly not easy.

Men, therefore, when saying their third blessing thanking God for not having made them a woman, are acknowledging two things: that they are held accountable for certain commandments and must, with humility, realize their accountability in that direction; and that the alternative of fewer commandments affords no greater ease and is therefore no more desirable.

A woman does not thank God for not having made her a male. She thanks Him for having "made me in accordance with His will." Rather than consoling her for the absence of the obligations only men are given, the woman's blessing is meant to instill in her the consciousness that no trimmings of masculinization are necessary for her to achieve ultimate closeness to God. A woman's spiritual "style" would be severely cramped were she forced to do everything on a man's terms.

Since women are exempt from most positive time-bound commandments, this puts most of their spiritual path into the category of areas of spiritual activity in which one uses one's own authority, as opposed to actions for which there is a specific legal mode of behavior. Every individual, male or female, is constantly confronted by the need to make choices for which one cannot turn to the *Shulchan Aruch* (Code of Jewish Law).

The fact that a particular situation comes under this category does not mean that any possible behavior is as good as another. For example, there is no specific law about how warmly you should welcome a guest, nor is there a possible way of defining the amount of warmth in legal terms. Torah lays out in a general sense the goals that have to be met. Using one's own authority means that the person has to know herself and the others who are involved well enough to know what will be the best response to the given situation.

The absence of externally imposed structure in large areas of one's life similarly does not mean that doing anything with one's time is as good as doing anything else. Torah does not allow women more freedom because it expects less of them; on the contrary, it assumes that women are capable of finding equally growth-producing outlets for their energies on their own. A woman who stays in bed happily reading *People* magazine while her husband is praying in the synagogue is totally missing the boat; worse than that, she is failing to live up to God's expectations of her. The corollary to the belief that a woman does not need such obligations as communal prayer is not that she can instead do anything she pleases and still reap the same spiritual rewards as a man. Rather, she possesses the potential to make the best choices as to how she can optimally use her time and is accordingly given the opportunity to do so. The rest is up to her.

The biblical story of Rebecca giving water to Eliezer and his camels at the well illustrates exemplary action within this realm.

Rebecca had no obligation to give water to a stranger who seemed perfectly capable of taking care of himself; her overwhelming kindness had no legal prescription. It was precisely the spontaneity of her choice to do deeds of kindness, with its enormous spiritual import, that convinced Eliezer that she was the ideal woman to marry Isaac and become the next matriarch of the Jewish people.

Dealing with the choices put before us by having a sense of who God is, what He wants, and what connection can be made to Him at any given moment comprises the essence of using one's own authority.

Career Choices

A woman's career should also be part of her spiritual life; otherwise she is spending most of her day at cross-purposes with her essential direction and goal. The choice of a career, therefore, must also be regarded from a spiritual perspective.

The Jewish view has always been that what you are as a person is infinitely more important than what you do for a living. A friend of mine read her Class Notes in the Yale alumni magazine. The entries were on the order of "Barbara Allen is working at Chancey and Harrington law firm," or "Arnold Murphy is working at First International Bank." She was tempted to write in, "Marilyn Manolson is working at becoming a better person."

We are all familiar with stories of men who sacrifice their families or their integrity (or both) in order to climb the corporate ladder. The evils of such prioritizing are clear; not so obvious is the merit of the inverse priority: to choose to become a better person or a better parent even if that entails limiting or sacrificing one's career. A generation ago, fathers who spent so much time at work that they were not there for their children were branded as cultural villains. Today a woman who puts her children in day care while she spends most of their waking hours at the office is considered liberated. In fact, the priorities – and the lingering resentment on the part of the children – are exactly the same.

. No one today remembers who was number 6 of the top ten U.S. businessmen in 1921 because it is not really all that important. (Who was President Harding's secretary of state? Who was the richest man in England in Disraeli's time? Who cares?) What we do still feel is the influence of the human values passed on to us by our own great-grandparents and their ancestors. The value systems they lived by, not the careers they selected, are their eternal imprint. If making one's years comprise a life of enduring meaning is one's priority, then career obviously cannot be the ultimate parameter of success. Few things can be as pathetic as an obituary that reads, "Known primarily for her significant contributions to the field of corporate management."

Given that she views it in the appropriate perspective, a Jewish woman's choice of career must depend on two things beyond her religious observance: her individuality and her womanhood. Both generic and gender-specific aspects of identity have to be confronted, just as they would for a man.

As Maimonides said, an individual can work in almost any profession that is permitted in a way in which he or she can maintain consciousness of God. If you are a computer programmer, and your basic intention is to provide someone with an honest, precise, and well-executed program, then you are being a giver in the same way as God. Conversely, if your intention is to contribute as little as possible and to get as much as possible for yourself, the part of you that is a taker becomes strengthened moment by moment.

In terms of the particulars of choosing a profession, the author of the medieval classic *Duties of the Heart* recommends that one ask oneself four questions: What am I drawn to? What is actually available? What would benefit the community at this time? What would draw me closer to God? These criteria are valid for both men and women. You have to see what really interests you based on your talents and look at what is really out there instead of fantasizing about a lifestyle that may or may not exist. Also, you should consider what would benefit the community in which you live. Finally, you have to be aware of the distinct nature of your own spirituality. You have to explore who you are and what you are, and that includes being a woman.

Any young woman who hopes to be married and a mother one day (or already is) must be particularly careful and realistic in her choice of career. The demands certain careers (such as airline pilot) place on one's time and energy would make maintaining any semblance of a real family life very difficult. This would therefore pose serious problems for anyone, woman or man, who does not want work to eclipse spouse and children. While there are a few genuine "superwomen" who somehow manage to do it all and be it all, the limitations of time and energy usually mean that the world-famous brain surgeon who is on call for his or her patients will not be equally available to family.

Fortunately, with current life expectancies, a woman can have sequential careers, giving priority to her family while her children are young and dependent and still have twenty or thirty years left to pursue another career of her choice afterward. Numerous career options exist even during the period of child-rearing for those of us who do not want to devote our entire lives to our jobs yet want a satisfying and serious occupation outside the home.

A woman should aim to maintain consciousness of the feminine quality of *tzniut* in her profession. While she can engage in many careers without losing her essentially internal self-definition, certain careers may entail a compromise of *tzniut* and thus jeopardize the focus of her spiritual development. Our actions affect our personalities over the course of time whether or not we choose to be affected. When a person selects a career in which salary is commensurate with loss of privacy or spiritual self-definition, she must ultimately live with who she has become and the sacrifices she made in the process. Many highly public positions (such as actress or anchorwoman) inevitably engender certain intrusions into one's being, especially if one's orientation is more internal from the start. While such jobs are not technically forbidden to women, they may not be a choice that a woman for whom *tzniut* is a priority would view as best for herself.

To the degree that the generalization of woman's use of insight holds true for an individual, she might want to choose a career that would make use of and further develop this intellectual capacity (such as clinical psychology, education, personnel work). Nevertheless, a woman who wishes to pursue a very analysis-oriented career (such as secular law) is not necessarily compromising her development in other, more spiritual realms.

For those who fear that the religious lifestyle leaves women no creative career outlets, I should mention that in the Orthodox community in Jerusalem I am acquainted with female doctors, artists, authors, social workers, craftswomen, businesswomen, designers, heads of large institutions, and one veterinarian.

Rosh Chodesh

Rosh Chodesh (day of the new moon), marking the first day of the Jewish month, is considered a special holiday for women. On this day they generally refrain from certain mundane tasks such as laundry and sewing and often arrange special women's gatherings, such as classes, musical events, and festive potluck get-togethers. In many communities, groups of friends get together on the first day of each Hebrew month to eat, learn, or share with each other.

It is significant that the commandment to sanctify the new moon was the first ordinance given to the Jews as a people while they were still in Egypt. The Midrash tells us that a certain type of light was needed to alleviate the darkness of the exiles that the Jewish people would be subjected to in the future. Our ability to renew ourselves nationally flows from the consciousness contained in this commandment. A closer look at the process will explain this.

Historically Rosh Chodesh was determined not simply by the moon's reappearance but by its formal recognition by the Supreme Court of the Jewish nation. Each month witnesses would come before the court and declare that they had seen the first sliver of the new moon. The court would then rule that a new month had begun. Sanctification of the new moon therefore entailed the Jewish people's placing itself above the physical world by assuming authority for the declaration of time. In so doing, they implicitly imbued a new month with sanctity.

In a similar way, we can bring holiness to any time and place by virtue of our faith in God as the One who transcends space and time. This faith ultimately manifests itself in the capacity for spiritual regeneration. Rosh Chodesh is seen as a symbol of this ever-renewing light, representing faith in times of exile and oppression.

Emunah (trust), the strong sense of God's Presence in the world, is what made us worthy of being redeemed from our first exile in Egypt and was expressed predominantly by the women. They instilled in the children of each subsequent generation their distinct identity despite the pressures to assimilate the values of the surrounding Egyptian culture. We are told that we were saved from becoming Egyptians of Hebrew ethnicity by virtue of the fact that we did not change our names, our clothing, or our language. These three aspects of self-definition are determined for children primarily by their mothers.

The same faith prevented the Jewish women in the desert from joining in the sin of the golden calf. This transgression was the result of an understandable psychological need, felt acutely by many of the men, to have everything within the known rules of nature, i.e., time and space. Moses was on Mount Sinai not only for the forty days for which he had prepared the people, but for an additional six hours. This was sufficient time for the faith of those who saw reality in overwhelmingly physical terms to falter. The women, whose view of life left more room for the transcendent, were steadfast enough not to doubt God or Moses but rather to doubt the veracity of human calculation.

In the merit of their faith, culminating in their refusal to participate in the sin of the golden calf, women were rewarded with their special relationship to Rosh Chodesh, which celebrates the meeting of the physical (time) with the transcendent (holiness).

Women's celebrations of the new month highlight a sociological phenomenon in the religious world that is often noticed by outsiders: the large proportion of time that religious women spend in the company of other females. Women could almost be considered a nation within a nation. This reflects a sense of sisterhood and shared experience that is very vitalizing.

When a woman enters the religious world, one of the first things she usually notices is the comparative absence of cattiness or more covert petty jealousies among the women. These, unfortunately, all too often characterize societies in which women value themselves primarily in terms of their desirability to men and hence find themselves viewing one another as competitors for male attention.

Sisterhood is epitomized in the Torah by the Hebrew midwives in Egypt. Their commitment to other women and their children came from a place of highly developed empathy and compassion. This stemmed, in turn, from an awareness of the bonds created by sharing female experiences (in their case, birthing under the conditions imposed by the Egyptians).

Today, too, those women who are most sensitive to the uniqueness of feminine experience, whether seen as resulting from biological, sociological, or other realities, have the strongest sense of sisterhood. The deep appreciation for life as lived and experienced Jewishly is what creates the observable closeness and feeling of community among religious women.

Learning Torah

In every age and in every country Jewish women have learned Torah. The vast majority of Jewish women throughout the ages knew more of the written and oral law, including the Pentateuch, laws, and parts of the Talmud than 90 percent of American Jewish women today. One would have been hard-pressed either in eighth-century Babylonia or in eighteenth-century Poland to find a single Jewish woman who did not know the names of the twelve tribes of Israel or the basic laws of keeping the Shabbat. In those social and economic strata where the men were literate, so were the women, at least in the Hebrew alphabet, which was also used to write Yiddish. In Eastern Europe, special books, such as prayer books in Hebrew with Yiddish commentaries, were published for women.

This does not mean that women spent their days as many men did, in formal learning in houses of study, but they were replete with what Western educators today would call "life credits." Since everyone was expected to observe the commandments, Jews had to be educated in the many laws that shaped their lives. Just as any secular teenager today can reel off the names of the twenty top rappers and websites, Jewish girls were conversant with all the biblical characters and the names of the sages up to their own times. In Jewish society, ignorance was never considered a virtue for anyone.

In non-Orthodox circles today, the fact that women do not learn Talmud is seen as discrimination. We can understand this issue in depth by exploring not only the nature of the Talmud, but the purpose of the positive commandment to learn Torah at set times every day, which applies to men but not to women.

The purpose of performing any commandment is to develop a closer connection to the Infinite. This is equally true with regard to learning any aspect of Torah. Whatever intellectual development is experienced and whatever understandings are acquired are a means to reaching a point of spiritual consciousness that entails true awe of God. Awe can be experienced only through the soul. For wisdom to be translated into awe of God, therefore, its final destination must be not the mind but the soul.

The Talmud comprises two approaches. One approach is legal (the *halachah*, which literally means "the path that is walked"); the other is *aggadah*, a very loose term that includes everything else — parables, history, philosophy. About 90 percent of the Talmud is devoted to legalities, and only about 10 percent to *aggadah*.

The legalistic side of the Talmud devotes itself to defining the road God requires people to walk in all areas of life: business, eating, agriculture. Its approach is that of detached logical argument.

The aggadic side similarly exposes God's will; however, its approach, whether in the stories or in ethical dictums, is aimed at giving as deep a picture as possible. The methodology is based less on argument than on peeling away various levels of the issues involved to gain a profound understanding of them.

Women have always learned the ethical and moral sections of the Talmud such as *Pirkei Avot* (Chapters of the Fathers) and were familiar with the parables and allegory. This corresponds both to their interests and to their specific abilities.

The legal parts of the Talmud, which comprise the vast majority of its contents, are addressed almost exclusively to the analytical approach. Success in studying most of the Talmud involves rigorous examination and reexamination of the details of the text. It demands objectivity about the topic being studied. In terms of spiritual direction, such study is not viewed as the vehicle by which women are most likely to achieve the end goal – the opening of the soul.

Insight, woman's optimal means of opening that gate, is not nurtured from the detached analysis required by typical Talmudic study. Total involvement rather than total detachment is what causes insight to flourish. The statement that women are exempt from learning Talmud implies that their specific path of study can be as profound in its effect as any other.

Ideally, much of true wisdom, especially that which relates to women, is more effectively conveyed by human beings than books. When my children were young, I sent them to a Yiddish-speaking nursery school operated by a young woman of about sixteen who had very little scholarship but was very good with children. On one occasion she had reason to rebuke me. Most likely she had studied neither the Codes nor the Talmud, but she knew exactly how the Torah requires one to administer rebuke (that is, Maimonides's four conditions: privacy, being specific, not to speak from anger or with intention to hurt, and only if the rebuke is likely to be accepted). How did she know this? In her society she no doubt had not seen anyone whom she respected offer rebuke in any other manner.

Today very few people grow up in a society in which one can absorb wisdom through observation. As various aspects of society progressively disintegrate, more and more has to be learned from books, because less is accessible through life itself. A book such as Maurice Lamm's *The Jewish Way in Death and Mourning*, for example, is surely not one that any contemporary of Rabbi Lamm's grandmother would have had to read.

Given the present state of society, there are no major Jewish schools of thought that would exclude women from academic study; rather, such study is highly encouraged. Indeed, if it is the only means of acquiring necessary knowledge, it is required. Today especially, formal education for girls is considered vital to the fabric of Jewish society. This is evidenced by the responsa of one of the great rabbis of the previous generation. He states that in times (such as ours) when faith is weak, one must give precedence to girls' education over that of boys, since it is Jewish women who hold the key to the spiritual survival of the Jewish people.

Care, however, must be given to pattern the material studied after the spiritual realities of the person learning. Studying texts that deepen and broaden insight, such as the Bible or the philosophical works, be they ethically or mystically oriented, is more relevant to most women because they address their need to hear an answer to why.

Certain individual women are more oriented toward analytical study. If it is clear that such a woman needs to learn Talmud to achieve her full spiritual growth, she is allowed to do so. What is not acceptable is for the type of Torah study that is aimed at the majority of women to be disdained because it is less "masculine."

For whatever a woman chooses to study, she is rewarded. If a man (even her father) implies that his way alone is valid, this is wrong and possibly immoral; at best, it is patronizing.

The Bais Yaakov movement (founded by Sarah Schenirer in

the early 1900s) is a primary example of a school system in which there is serious commitment to educating women without stifling either their intellectuality or their femininity. The rabbinical leadership accordingly has supported it since its inception. Today especially, it and other schools like it represent a refreshing departure from the "If you want to do it right, do it like a man" mentality.

If we understand this difference in intellectual proclivity and development, we will understand why the Orthodox community has separate schools for boys and girls. Schools for girls generally emphasize more conceptual growth and the acquisition of a particular outlook on religious life, while schools for boys are usually oriented more toward gaining textual skills.

Another reason for separate education is to allow learning to take place without the distraction of the opposite sex. In the average co-ed high school or college, a good deal of the attention and energy that should be devoted to learning goes into trying to impress the opposite sex. While this becomes a serious concern only as children approach adolescence, boys and girls in the religious community are generally separated from a young age for the sake of establishing general mores for the future.

No exposition of the spiritual path of Jewish women would be complete without a discussion of two of its central practices, marriage and motherhood, which are seen as paths to spiritual perfection no less than the more obvious spiritual practices such as prayer. These subjects, however, require chapters of their own.

Six

Marriage

The first commandment that God gave Adam, to be fruitful and multiply, is a positive precept incumbent on Jewish men. They must marry and produce at least one son and one daughter. Jewish women are not obligated in this precept, for several reasons.

Until the advent of modern medicine, childbirth presented a very real threat to a woman's life. The Torah, whose "paths are paths of pleasantness and its ways are [those of] peace," would not command a woman to endanger herself as part of the normal course of living. The major reason, however, for not obligating women in this precept is that being married and mothering have always been so much a part of the female identity that making it mandatory would be much like telling a bird to fly or a fish to swim.

In the 1970s and early '80s, this last statement would have been hotly contested. The women's liberation movement (as discussed in chapter 1) convinced many women that their fulfill-ment and happiness lay in careers rather than in marriage and motherhood. As the '90s approached, however, we saw these same women, now in their thirties and early forties, rushing to have children before the onset of menopause.

Fertility clinics specializing in "over thirty-five-year-olds," paying five-figure fees to accomplish what would probably have been easy at twenty-five, have proliferated. In uptown Manhattan, maternity stores and children's clothing shops have mush-roomed, and the phenomenon of the "menopausal mom" has re-ceived wide media coverage.

Even more significant is the often surprised delight these women take in their experience of motherhood. A friend of mine traveled in the Far East four times, wrote a book, and adminis-tered a large organization. At the age of forty she married, gave birth to her first child, and exclaimed, "Having a baby is the best thing I ever did in my life!"

Marriage, from a Jewish perspective, is a spiritual endeavor. A woman who succeeds in this venture not only has a partner with whom to split the work and go on vacations, but she herself is transformed through the disciplines and challenges of marriage. With the current divorce rate in the secular world at 50 to 60 per-cent (in the Orthodox Jewish world, it is 15 to 20 percent), it would be worthwhile to explore the Torah's concept of what the marriage partnership entails.

Ezer Kenegdo

The Torah clearly states (Genesis 2:20) that woman was cre-ated to be an "*ezer kenegdo*," helpmate, who is parallel or opposite man. At the time of woman's creation, the first human was living a paradisiacal existence that required no physical assistance: he wore no clothes (no laundry), and his food was readily available (no shopping and cooking). The assistance for which woman was created, therefore, was of a purely spiritual nature. Woman was to help man reach his growth potential, thereby achieving her own as well.

After Adam and Eve made their fatal mistake in the Garden of Eden, they entered into a state of existence that was fraught with not only spiritual but physical challenges. Although woman's role as helper necessarily expanded to assist him in these new areas, her fundamental raison d'être did not change.

This is not to say that woman does not benefit from man's spiritual and physical assistance as well. A woman, for example, is seen as "helping" her husband by relieving him of the primary responsibility of the home and children so that he can engage in other activities. Yet first and foremost among these activities is providing an income for the household so that his wife is free to experience the rewards of bringing up her children.

Clearly, much of the giving within a marriage relationship is of a reciprocal nature. Indeed, in any healthy relationship there should be a give-and-take on all levels. Yet implicit in the wife being called the "helpmate" is the idea that the woman has a larger contribution to make to the man's spiritual completion than the man to the woman's.

King Solomon, the wisest person who ever lived, authored a famous poem entitled *Eishet Chayil* (A Woman of Valor), the last chapter of the book of Proverbs. Among the verses extolling the virtues of the ideal Jewish woman we find, about halfway through the poem, a seemingly unrelated sentence that appears to praise not the woman but her husband: "Her husband is known [distinctive] in the gates [councils], when he sits with the elders of the land." The statement implicit in the inclusion of this verse is that the woman is to be given credit for what her husband has become.

Since God wants both men and women to reach their spiritual potential, He created woman with the nature to thrive emotionally and attain spiritual completion through being a "helpmate." The woman, therefore, both desires more to help and grows more through the experience than her husband.

In Judaism, the fact that one person is the helper and the other is being helped implies nothing derogatory about the value of either. Each is important solely to the degree of significant contribution toward achieving their mutual goal. Being a helper entails devoting one's attention primarily to the process involved in achieving an end. While the person being helped is the one who externally accomplishes the goal, it is the helper who makes its realization possible – in itself a valid goal.

A pilot and a navigator, for example, are two equally educated professionals who work together to achieve a desired end. While one flies the plane and the other helps by advising in which direction to go, they are equally important in getting the plane to its destination. A doctor who is helping a patient may be primarily or even solely responsible for achieving a cure, whereas the person being helped may be able to contribute very little. The relative importance of the helpmate within the male-female relationship likewise derives not from the role definition as such but from what one does (or does not do) within the role.

Who's the Boss?

Unfortunately, literary stereotypes have distorted our generation's view of the Jewish woman's role within marriage. *Fiddler
on the Roof*, for many of its viewers their sole source of information on Eastern European Jewish history or traditions, conveyed
the image of the man as the master and the woman as the obedient, subservient partner. This is a gross distortion of both the historical reality and the legal ground rules. A man is not the master
of his wife in the same way that he is the owner of his possessions.

The relationship between a man and a woman, called *kinyan*,
meaning "acquisition," is not comparable to the acquisition of
goods. If you buy a roll of Scotch tape, for example, you can use it
as you please — destroy it, give it away — because you own it. This
is certainly not the way Jewish law views a man's relationship to
his wife. He cannot buy her, destroy her, give her away, or abuse
her. Acquisition in this case means not that he owns her, but that
she belongs to him like himself. She becomes part of his self-
definition, and he in turn becomes an aspect of hers.

Ideally neither partner should have to assume the role of
boss in a marriage. The relationship between husband and wife
should be such that agreement can be reached on most, if not all,
important family issues. Where this is not the case, Jewish law
views certain areas of life as being the primary domain of the man
and others as that of the woman.

The basic division of authority in the home is that the man
has the final word in "things of heaven," those having to do with
the religious aspects of the home (such as what schools the children should attend, which customs should be practiced); the

woman is in charge of "things of earth," all practical matters involved in the home. Each of these is an equally valuable spiritual contribution. While men may have more sensitivity to the specifics of the Torah's dictates, most women can intuitively sense how to use everyday material things toward spiritual ends. The ability to create a physical environment that articulates spiritual values is specifically feminine.

The woman's authority over the day-to-day requirements of the home reflects her greater ability to understand the fluidity of individual needs (such as what type of physical environment will affect whom in which way and when), as opposed to the ability to apply legal criteria of limited flexibility to specific problems.

The concept of elevation of the physical is central to Judaism. The clarity of vision needed to take the ideals of the higher worlds and give them a physical address empowers the possessor of this insight. Men are told explicitly in the Talmud to listen to the council of their wives in practical matters. Since the real world is our venue, this implies a major statement about power. The Torah ideal is that of two people bonded together as one unit with a common identity and commitment, but with different and equally important areas of authority. Cooperation is the expected norm, and a marriage in which tension and dispute lead either partner to cut off the conversation with "It's my right to decide" is not desirable.

We can now begin to understand the Talmudic statement "A proper wife does the will of her husband." This certainly does not mean that she should be his obedient servant — there is no justification for such a chauvinistic reading. Rather, we must delve deeper to understand the Judaic meaning of *will*, a major theological concept.

A person's deepest will is identical to God's highest will for him or her. The idea that ultimately people want to do what is right in God's eyes is reflected in the Hebrew word for will, *ratzon*, which is composed of the same three letters as *tzinor*, "channel" or "conduit." A person's deepest will is a conduit for the Divine will. (This premise is reflected in Jewish law. A divorce is considered valid only if the husband gives it willingly. The rabbinical court is allowed, however, to beat him until he verbalizes his desire to grant it. Such coercion seems to conflict with the premise of his giving the divorce willingly. This conflict is resolved with the explanation that it is man's deepest will to do what is right in the eyes of God. When he says, "I want...," he is verbalizing this inner yearning.)

The effective helper works in terms of the true needs of the person being aided. A wife must therefore help her husband recognize how he can become a conduit for the Divine will in his individual life – to help him serve God, not his own ego. Doing "her husband's will" does not mean giving in to whims that will take him away from his truest and best self. A woman whose husband asks her to help him do something that is forbidden by the Torah, for example, should obviously not oblige him.

Thus Rashi, the foremost biblical commentator, explains the meaning of *helpmate*, which in the original Hebrew literally translates as "a helper against him." "If he is worthy," says Rashi, "she is a helper; if he is not worthy, she is against him." While a husband may want to be simply what he is, a wife must want him to be what he can be. At the same time, she must be realistic enough to address herself not to the ideal self that she would like her husband to personify, but to who he really is capable of being and honor that person and his potential.

This does not mean that a wife should be her husband's mentor; that would connote condescension, which is not intended here. Positive change cannot happen through nagging or confrontation, but, as a supportive equal, she can help him find and express his deepest will.

A wife has the power to affect her husband positively or negatively. I know a woman whose husband, though neither a noted scholar nor a great financial success, is a warmhearted and generous person. She made sure that plaques lauding his generosity to various institutions were placed in prominent places in their home. One can almost feel this man's self-esteem rise when he walks into his house. Conversely, a wife who does not give her husband the kind of honor he needs to develop his confidence will find that her husband's truest will may not be actualized because he may not be aware of his own potential.

Because a woman generally possesses a larger natural endowment of insight, she has access to a correspondingly greater understanding of her spouse. The chance that she will be able to influence her husband for the good is therefore much greater than his ability to affect her. On the other hand, in the Garden of Eden it was Eve whom the snake chose to approach rather than Adam on the assumption that she would more likely be able to persuade him to sin than vice versa. The ability to influence can be used for both beneficial and detrimental ends. This is the meaning of a well-known story in the Midrash.

There was once a righteous couple who divorced, and each subsequently remarried wicked people. The man became as wicked as his second wife, while the woman influenced her new husband to become righteous. The moral of the story, the Midrash concludes, is that "everything comes from the woman."

Beyond the idea of women's influence, there is another reality reflected in the one-sidedness of the statement that a wife should do her husband's will and not vice versa. While all people need both respect and love, for most women the need for love is the stronger of the two. Men, on the other hand, generally have a greater emotional need to be respected in the specific sense of being looked up to. (One might not like this reality, but it is true nonetheless and deeply ingrained as well.)

Sociologically one could attribute this in some measure to the different avenues through which the two sexes are able to develop much of their sense of self. A major part of a woman's essential identity, her capacity to bear and nurture new life, is intrinsic to her being; a man must "find himself" largely in the world of outside achievements, whether career, study of Torah, or other accomplishments. Consequently, a man's sense of security in his purpose in life, and hence his self-esteem, is subject to greater risk, leading him to have a correspondingly greater need for acknowledgment.

On a psychological level, it has been noted that feminine identity entails attachment to others, while males achieve their sense of self ultimately through separation and individuation. Women therefore have a greater need for their husbands' love and men a greater need to be looked up to or respected as strong individuals (sometimes resulting in the famous "male ego").

Seen in a direct spiritual light, women's and men's respective needs reflect their intuitive realization of what they were created for: woman primarily to maintain the inner world of family and relationships, man to assume leadership in more external realms.

No matter what the source of the sexes' respective emotional makeups, there has to be recognition of each other's deep needs and a willingness not only to take but to give in order for a marriage to work. A sensitive husband who understands the nature of his wife's needs will make sure that she feels secure in his love. Indeed, numerous Jewish books addressed to men advise them, among other things, of the importance of this aspect of married life. Similarly, a woman's recognition of her husband's needs should help her to give the man she loves the respect he needs to grow. This is perhaps the greatest act of loving-kindness that a wife can bestow upon her husband.

A common misconception in contemporary culture is that a woman's nurturing of her husband and children is mutually exclusive of her fulfilling her own legitimate needs. This is usually voiced as the complaint "When will I find time for myself?" Yet we have seen that being a helpmate and nurturer actualizes a woman's own spiritual potential. As in all giving enterprises (social work, charity volunteering), one discovers that in aiding others one has actually benefited oneself. Therefore, when a woman engages in helping and nurturing activities, she reaps the rewards of correspondingly greater spiritual enrichment. Her own truest needs, rather than standing on the sidelines while she is busy helping others, are thus being actively satisfied by her other-directed actions.

We all have a multitude of our own legitimate requirements, however, which should not be ignored. This is the meaning of the oft-quoted maxim from *Pirkei Avot* (Chapters of the Fathers): "If I am not for myself, who will be for me? And if I am only for myself, what am I?"

Not every spiritual need of a woman can be fulfilled within the primary center for giving and nurturing, the home and family. Even involvement in community activities is not enough for some women, particularly those who have intellectual needs that cannot be satisfied by even the most enchanting discussion with a precocious three-year-old.

A Jewish woman, no less than any other, must be honest about all of her real needs and talents and find appropriate and satisfying outlets for them. For many women, although attention to their children and maintaining a relationship with their husbands is their first priority, this means formal Torah or secular studies, work outside the home, or volunteer work. In addition to self-fulfillment, most Jewish women have much to offer the community and the world at large and should take advantage of the opportunities available to them.

Within the roles of helpmate and nurturer themselves, a woman must also be honest about her own personal requirements. Since needs vary, priority must be given to those that are at the time most objectively pressing. If you are tired, for example, a child's yearning for still another story might be real, but not as vital at that moment as your need to get sleep. In this case you will clearly have to put your own needs before those of the child.

Sometimes, however, the situation is not one of "their need" versus "my need," but "my need" versus "my need." For example, in the winter, when Shabbat comes in very early and tensions during preparations run high, the desire to project yourself as an elegant hostess serving four kinds of homemade cake and your simultaneous need not to work yourself to a frazzle may directly conflict. As a working woman with guests coming to dinner you may find yourself in the same situation. You may think you are making the cakes for your guests, but self-evaluation will often reveal subtle ulterior motives. Questioning, "Is this a want, or is this a need?" and "Who am I helping by this?" can clear a lot of self-pity out of one's life. This is yet another aspect of taking care of oneself, which in this case means looking out for one's real self.

Adultery: Who Counts Most?

Several aspects of Jewish marriage law need to be understood in depth; otherwise a superficial understanding could lead to the fallacious conclusion – held by many feminists – that these laws are chauvinistic. A thorough investigation will reveal, however, that Torah laws concerning marriage reflect a deep understanding of the nature and needs of human beings, both male and female.

According to the Torah, the sin of adultery is so grave that a Jew must be willing to be killed rather than commit it. Of all the myriad precepts of the Torah, only two other sins share this worse-than-death status: murder and idol worship. One can (and must) violate the Shabbat, eat on Yom Kippur, or eat bread on Passover in order to save a life, including one's own. From a Torah perspective, however, it is better to die than to commit adultery, murder, or idol worship.

Each of these cardinal sins actually leads to a death. Murder is obviously the death of the body, idol worship for a Jew brings about the death of the soul, and adultery brings about the death of the basic social unit, the family, which ultimately leads to the death of society.

The Torah's definition of adultery is sexual relations between a married woman and a man who is not her husband (either married or single). If a single woman has relations with a man, either married or single, it is not considered adultery; if a married man has relations with a single woman, while this is forbidden, he has not committed the grave sin of adultery.

The Torah originally permitted (but not encouraged) polygyny in light of the psychological reality that men are generally able to carry on simultaneous relationships in a way that women are not. Accordingly, it should be clear that a man is capable of entering into an adulterous relationship that is so superficial that it does not affect his essence. (Indeed, the stereotypical reply of a husband to his upset wife's charge of infidelity is "But it meant nothing to me!" And this is quite likely true.) This is by no means to say that Judaism legalizes or even condones male infidelity, but simply that it recognizes different psychosexual realities for women and men.

For a woman, the act of sexual giving involves such totality of self that the effect of her infidelity on herself and her marriage is total. Thus, when a woman commits adultery, it is viewed as a complete breach of her marriage relationship. She has, in effect, destroyed the very relationship that she, as a woman, was primarily capable of creating and maintaining. This breach is so severe that, in a certain sense, it is second only to murder in terms of the damage it does to the couple's humanity.

The Torah describes a specific process (no longer practiced), called the "sotah ritual," for determining the guilt or innocence of a woman who, on convincing grounds, is suspected of adultery. In focusing here on the woman, the Torah presents her as the one who had the capacity and depth to realize, more than a man, what marriage could be.

If a husband had reasonable grounds to suspect that his wife had another man in her life, he had an obligation to warn her not to be alone with him. The term *sotah*, errant woman, refers only to a woman who, though warned by her husband, persists in being alone with this man behind closed doors.

Given that the wife continues to seclude herself with this man, she certainly is not behaving like an innocent woman. At best, she is not an adulteress. At the least, she is guilty of having taken lightly the depth and seriousness of what marriage should be, for both herself and her husband.

At this point, given that the evidence was highly unfavorable, it became forbidden for her to continue to have marital relations with her husband and either of them could opt for divorce. The woman was given ample opportunity to think over her deeds in order that she confess and accept a divorce. The entire narrative starts with the premise that the woman had insisted she was innocent, did not want a divorce, and, in order to again be permitted to her husband, chose to go through the *sotah* ritual.

The woman was brought to the Temple by the *beit din hagadol* (high court) in Jerusalem, where a unique ritual was enacted. She first presented an offering of barley meal (viewed then as animal food), symbolizing that she had given in to her lower desires in carrying on with another man. The officiating priest would remove her head covering, let down her hair, and tear her dress to symbolize the compromise of her dignity as a married woman. He would then list the curses that would befall her should she be found guilty, and she would swear to accept them. The curses, containing God's divine Name, would be written on a parchment and dissolved in water contained in an earthen vessel. This case of attempting to restore peace between husband and wife is, it should be noted, the only occasion in all of the Torah where it is permitted to erase the Name of God.

At any point in the process thus far, the woman could change her mind and accept the divorce. If she continued to maintain her innocence, she would then drink the water. This was meant to convey that by not using her earthly body for a spiritual purpose she had caused the Name of God to be erased. It was only after this that her options were closed and she could no longer accept a divorce.

Were she indeed guilty, she would die a death that was conspicuous and painful. This fate was simultaneously experienced by the man with whom she had had an affair — he suffered the same grotesque death, no matter where he was at the moment and without exception. On the other hand, if the woman was innocent, she experienced no physical effects. She returned to her husband and was blessed with children.

In terms of physical punishment, there was no difference between the woman and the man who had committed adultery. That the ritual centers on the woman reflects the Torah's general position that an individual's accountability for sin is directly proportionate to his or her spiritual potential in that same area.

The Structure of Jewish Marriage and Divorce

According to Jewish law, a man legally betroths a woman through transferring to her something of value (most commonly a ring) and making the pronouncement that she is herewith betrothed to him. When they marry, he presents her with a *ketubah* (marriage contract), in which his main marital obligations, and particularly his financial responsibility to her in the event of divorce, are stated explicitly. A woman does not present a man with something or make a statement to indicate her willingness to marry and to assume her responsibilities. The woman's willingness to fulfill her part as a wife is implied by her accepting the ring and the document.

This is in accordance with the general nature of legal contracting in Judaism, in which one party presents a contract to the other, whose acceptance of the contract implies agreement to the terms therein. In all Jewish contracting, one party plays an active role and the other a passive. That the Torah chose the husband to assume the active role is sourced in the understanding of the man as the one who actively pursues (or courts) the woman and whose nature dictates the need for more externally articulated commitments. These truths in turn reflect the concept of man being the external half of the whole that was the original Adam.

The idealized state of what a divorce should be (if we can talk about idealized states in divorce) is one in which there is mutual consent. Almost always, if the people involved are honest, this agreement will exist. Very few people want to hold on to a marriage that is a failure. While it is possible that an emotionally sick person may not cooperate just to spite the other, in the overwhelming majority of cases where one party is refusing a divorce, the refusal is based on an unsatisfactory financial settlement rather than a desire to stay in the relationship.

In the case of mutual consent, obtaining a divorce is a simple and straightforward procedure. The husband and wife appear before a rabbinical court, which urges them to see if there is any way in which they can achieve a harmonious and productive relationship. If there is not, they may divorce. The enactment of the divorce parallels the way in which the marriage was begun: the man hands the woman his express and written document, called a "*get*," and states that he is herewith divorcing her. The man presents the *get* to the woman as he is the one who presented the ring and contract at the beginning of the marriage.

More importantly, that the man must actively present the document eliminates any possibility of ambiguity as to whether he has indeed divorced his wife. This clarity is more crucial for the woman than for the man because original Torah law permitted a man to take more than one wife. Therefore, a married man is not technically committing adultery if he has relations with another woman who herself is not married (although it is forbidden and grounds for divorce), while a woman's remarriage or sexual relationship subsequent to a legally invalid divorce would constitute adultery.

Lack of mutual consent can create problems. While the court can order a divorce, it does not actually enact it; this must be done by the two parties themselves. A woman cannot unilaterally declare herself divorced, nor can a man toss his wife a document and say goodbye. Each has equal power to refuse to let the marriage be terminated. Where agreement and cooperation are lacking, long waits may ensue, and the field is open for manipulation and exploitation.

My husband and I know a man, for example, who is a tradesman of modest means (certain facts are disguised). He wanted a divorce from his wife, not because he had serious and concrete grounds against her, but because he found it impossible to live with her extremely difficult personality. She, for her part, was not honest with herself about the reason for the marriage's failure. Since personality issues alone do not constitute the kind of objective, definable grounds that would make termination of the marriage a legal imperative, the court could not order her to accept the divorce. Therefore, in exchange for accepting the document, she was able to force him into making incredibly high child-support payments in addition to buying her an apartment. The result is that he was left in a situation where for all intents and purposes he is financially tied down to her for the rest of his life, and his ability to support a second wife and family was practically nil.

Similarly, there are instances in which a man could tell his wife, "Sure, I'll give you a divorce, as long as you let me take all of our savings and release me from having to give you more than ten dollars a month."

Even in cases where divorce is objectively called for, and the court does order either party to give or accept it, the parties can simply ignore the order. Today's religious courts, both in Israel and the diaspora, cannot ensure compliance with their orders because the civil authorities will neither enforce the rabbis' dictates nor grant the religious courts themselves the power to do so. Even where there exist unarguable grounds for divorce, the rabbis can in effect do no more than say, "You really should accept this divorce" or "You really should give this divorce." Therefore, if an individual acts outside of Torah law in choosing not to listen to the rabbis, there is no legal way of forcing him or her to do so.

Given the tragic number of *agunot* (women who have been abandoned by their husbands without receiving a divorce) in the world today — and even one would be a tragic number — many concerned people ask why the law cannot be changed to allow a woman to give the document. They do not realize that this would not solve the problem of a recalcitrant husband, since the man could still refuse to accept it even if the court were to order him to do so.

While Torah law grants women equal power to refuse a divorce, there are clearly more cases of women who are "stuck" and unable to get a divorce from their husbands than the opposite. This undoubtedly reflects the reality that the woman very often has more extensive and sophisticated needs in the relationship that her husband may be unable to satisfy. At the same time (and largely because of this), it is generally she who is more perceptive in recognizing that a relationship cannot succeed. Consequently, she will often be the one who wants out, while he can't understand what the problem is, and therefore it is she who finds herself at the mercy of an embittered husband.

For a man whose wife will not accept a divorce, there is an obscure and difficult loophole by which he could at least marry another woman. Under very specific and extreme circumstances (for example, if his wife leaves him), a man today could theoretically obtain "*heter mei'ah rabbanim*" (permission granted through a hundred rabbis). This does not permit him to divorce this wife against her will — no one can permit that — but it permits him to marry another woman, since polygyny, as we have said, was not originally forbidden by the Torah.

Now, getting a hundred rabbis to agree that the sky is blue is not an easy task, especially given the fragmentation in the religious world today. Certainly to persuade a hundred rabbis to examine a case in the hope that they would unanimously decide to permit a man to marry a second woman is not something a man would undertake for frivolous reasons. Furthermore, this option is usually not open to Sefardic men, since their marriage contracts generally contain a clause prohibiting their taking of another wife, a necessary inclusion given the absence of a rabbinical ban on polygyny among Sefardic Jewry.

Since a woman was never permitted to take two husbands, she has no possibility of "permission from a hundred rabbis." So what should happen in the case of a husband who refuses to give his wife a divorce, even though he is not maintaining the conditions of the marriage contract or is a disreputable person or is having affairs with other women or is abusing her?

In clear-cut circumstances such as these, Jewish law empowers the rabbis to have the man beaten by the deputy of the court until he says that he wants to divorce his wife. This is in fact what would happen in former times, when the rabbis' power was not curtailed by the civil authorities. Today, social, economic, or sometimes even physical pressure will often be brought to bear against the husband by members of the community. If these measures fail or cannot be used, however, a woman may sometimes end up waiting for long periods of time for a divorce that her husband is not willing to give her.

As tragic as this situation of the stranded wife is, it is hardly the fault of the rabbinical courts. When the hands of the rabbis are tied behind their backs, one cannot blame them for their failure to achieve satisfactory results. This situation is equivalent to having a secular society eliminate prisons and fines and just instruct people to please not kill, please not steal, please not double-park, and please not walk against the red light. The solution to the problem lies in returning real power to the hands of the rabbis, allowing them to administer physical punishment or at least to force the recalcitrant husband to give a divorce through other compelling means.

In the United States, where civil marriages are more easily dissolved (because the secular courts can enact a divorce on the merits of one party's claims, irrespective of the other's unwillingness), one finds no fewer tragedies. One of the social consequences of taking the marriage bond so much more lightly, and particularly as a result of "no-fault" divorce, has been the "feminization of poverty." There has arisen a new class of female poor, divorced by husbands who, for example, "fell in love" with other (often younger) women and then were not able, willing, or even required to provide financial support to their ex-wives and children.

In other situations, where the husband finds himself divorced against his wishes and paying alimony and child support to boot, he is sure to feel short-changed. As a result, the ex-husband fails to pay what the court awarded his ex-wife and children. In the late 1980s, *Newsweek* reported that over 50 percent of children from divorced families in America received no child support at all from their fathers, despite court orders. Two decades and endless court battles later, the picture is, if anything, even grimmer.

Beyond the severe difficulties many women encounter in supporting a family alone, years of interminable legal fighting to receive overdue payments take an inestimable emotional toll. I know one American lawyer who spent over $100,000 in legal fees to get her former husband to pay his share of their children's college tuitions.

In short, the oppressive financial and emotional situation ensuing from an ex-husband's recalcitrance is not solved by a system that permits unilateral divorce. Insisting that there be a basic willingness on both sides, as the Torah demands, goes a long way toward ensuring that after the divorce has taken place resentment will not prevent the husband from following through financially. The process will then be over, making it possible for both parties to go on with their lives.

Any broken marriage is a tragedy. Being victim to another's exploitation or manipulations adds to it. Rewriting Jewish law will not erase the core of the problem, which is usually a form of selfishness, the magnitude of which precludes any simple adjustment in the law as a remedy.

An often repeated accusation against the Rabbinate is "Where there is a rabbinic will, there is a legal way." This implies that Jewish law is infinitely malleable, a premise that fails to recognize the realities of the legal process. The rabbinical function of interpreting and applying Torah law is based on the acknowledgment that the Torah itself issues from an immutable divine source. One of the commandments is to obey the injunctions of the rabbis — their interpretation of the law is built into the Torah itself. Clearly, if God had wanted every law to be black and white and to give us the answer to every question that could ever arise, Moses could have come down from Mount Sinai with a huge van of microchips. Rather, God saw value in having every question asked and answered through human authority.

The rules for interpreting Torah law, however, are very strictly defined. How much human loss and suffering can be a relevant factor in any decision is also strictly defined. Consider the question as to whether or not a quantity of food is kosher. There is a minority opinion in the Talmud that if it is not and a significant financial loss would ensue, the rabbi judging the matter can declare the food permissible in order to prevent the loss.

If, however, a whole warehouse full of paper money, the entire fortune of a person who has spent his whole lifetime to earn it, goes up in flames on Shabbat, there is absolutely no way of permitting the fire to be put out. No matter how much the owner and his family will suffer from the loss, there is no valid legal opinion in any of the sources that permits putting out a fire on Shabbat, an action specifically prohibited by the Torah.

Thus, while the rabbis are permitted to rely on a Talmudic minority opinion, they are not permitted to simply make up a new opinion that never existed in Jewish law. There can be "a legal way" only if there is a concrete and definable source in Torah law. Accordingly, the rabbis cannot permit either unilateral divorce or "permission from a hundred rabbis" for a woman to take a second husband, because there is no valid source for either practice anywhere in Jewish law.

The most difficult problem caused by the prohibitions of unilateral divorce and polyandry ensues when a husband is missing or not mentally competent to give a divorce, leaving the woman a true *agunah*, legally anchored in the marriage. These tragedies, while exceedingly rare, are the price that is paid in Judaism for two things: regarding marriage as so binding that mutual consent is required to dissolve it and recognizing that women's capacity for exclusivity in a relationship is too great to permit the compromise of a second coexisting relationship, even when the first no longer exists in the physical sense but only in spiritual terms.

Judaism is well aware of the possibility of a woman being without recourse as a result of these aspects of Jewish law. In specific circumstances, preventive measures may be taken. Soldiers, for example, often go to war knowing that they might not return and that their deaths might nevertheless not be technically verifiable (i.e., "missing in action"). Such a man could, upon leaving, give his wife a conditional divorce to be effective retroactive to the date of his departure should he not return within a specified amount of time. This practice was followed as early as the times of King David.

To further avoid the situation of the abandoned woman, the Talmud adopted various leniencies in ascertaining a husband's death. Primarily, it legislated that one witness instead of the two usually required could be relied upon to establish his demise. Testimony from a woman or a slave could also be accepted, as well as secondhand evidence.

In certain cases, a marriage could be retroactively annulled, obviating the need for a divorce altogether. Take, for example, if a husband's insanity (rendering him legally incompetent to give a divorce) could be attributed to a disease he had contracted prior to marriage. If his wife would not have married him had she known about it, the marriage could be ruled invalid, since she entered it without the full information necessary to make such a decision.

There are currently rabbis working on developing an acceptable formula for a prenuptial agreement that would require the husband to give a divorce under certain circumstances.

A significant difference in approach to the practice of Judaism exists between those who adhere to the traditional legal process and those who do not. Religious Jews idealize growth and movement toward Torah as their ultimate goal. Their universe is God-centered, and the Torah is understood to be the path toward gaining access to that core reality.

Non-Orthodox Jewish leaders, to one degree or another, see the world as human-centered. Rather than humans stretching themselves to the limits of their spiritual capacity by moving toward the Torah, seen as the definer of all values, non-Orthodox Jews see the Torah as a vehicle for adding depth and meaning to life. The Torah, therefore, is often made to "descend" to meet the people, rather than the people ascending to meet the Torah.

There are no limits to the elasticity of Torah once human society is the center. If feminism or any other ism is a social goal, then according to this view the Torah must somehow adjust itself to it. Presumably, if theft (or incest or any other act that the Torah forbids) were likewise to be a societal goal, the proponents of "where there's a rabbinic will, there's a legal way" would establish synagogues in which the "legitimate sharing of the world's goods by all people" could be popularized. (It is hard to imagine how to pull this off with incest, but how about the synagogue devoted to the "expression of legitimate multifaceted family love and intimacy"?)

Despite the rabbis' best efforts, there will be circumstances in which the law will not be able to declare an *agunah* free to remarry. Such a woman suffers greatly. Her avenues of succor, however, are spiritual, not legal.

The question rightfully asked about her pain is very much like the question we ask at the traditional Passover meal, the seder: Why on this night do we dip vegetables twice, once into salt water and once into *charoset*, a sweet mixture containing apples and wine? This twofold dipping alludes to the fact that the Jewish people's chosenness carries with it both the suffering of exile, represented by the salt water, a symbol of the tears shed in Egypt, and the sweetness of redemption.

As Jews, we have experienced God's intervention in our lives enough to recognize that our collective suffering has led ultimately to elevation and redemption. Redemption means not being defined by an outside source (a master, a political dictator, even a husband), but discovering and actualizing ourselves as a people and oneself as a person. We were created to meet challenges. The changes we undergo through confronting difficult realities open us up to growth. This is true not only collectively but individually.

We all would, at times, be happy to be a little less chosen, to have fewer opportunities to actualize our potential. We are only human. Yet part of being chosen — indeed, of being human — is the ability to get past the resistance to pain and change and allow them to move us toward becoming our best possible selves. This is true whether the difficulties are external to our souls (aging, illness, financial reverses) or whether they stem from the internal reality of our being a people who have a mission, such as when trying to keep Shabbat in the former Soviet Union or being an *agunah*, if that is where one's challenge lies.

I know a woman who has lived through such a challenge. At

the time I met her she was in her sixties and had come from Russia originally. Early in her marriage her young husband had been arrested and taken off to Siberia and was never heard from again. After many years passed, it became increasingly certain that he was not alive, yet she had no concrete proof of his death. In the end, she fled Russia in order to save her own life and those of her two small boys. As we became acquainted, I saw that her sons were well-adjusted, established adults and that she herself was one of the most independent and directed people I have ever met. I do not know what actually became of her husband or why God determined such a difficult course for her life. What was clear was that her life had meaning and depth and joy and that her experiences were part of the mosaic that had been constructed for her by God.

Seven

Motherhood

For women seeking a path of spiritual growth, challenge, and fulfillment, Judaism offers motherhood. In the past few decades (as we mentioned in chapter 1), many women have disdained the role, believing that bearing and raising children requires no particular intelligence or aptitude and that their talents are better spent in careers that will utilize their capabilities.

In truth, bearing and raising children well requires tremendous intelligence, creativity, character development, and insight. (Even the act of giving birth in an optimum way, as any Lamaze instructor will testify, requires research, acquired skills, and the ability to make informed choices.) In addition, Judaism regards motherhood as a spiritual practice of the highest order. It offers the potential for exercising a human being's highest capacity: *imitatio deo*, imitating God, by creating and giving according to the divine prototype.

The Torah has always presented the birth of children as a blessing. The letters of the Hebrew root word of *berachah*, blessing, are *beit*, *reish*, and *chaf*, which imply expansion and growth. In the system of letter-number equivalents (*gematriah*), *beit* equals 2, the first plural of the ones; *reish* equals 200, the first plural of the hundreds; and *chaf* equals 20, the first plural of the tens. Being blessed thus means being expanded. The ultimate human experience of expansion and creativity comes through childbearing and child-rearing. Helping a good human being to develop is the ultimate gift anyone could bestow upon the world.

The biblical figure Deborah, who was a prophetess and leader of the Jewish army against their Canaanite enemy, in some circles today would be endlessly honored for being "more than just someone's mother." Yet Deborah herself, in the song marking her victory, gives herself the accolade "a mother in Israel." While she saw her role as a political and military leader to be an exigency of the time, she did not thrive on the public status and power of her position. Her interest always remained directed toward sustaining and nurturing the people whose lives were in her care.

Any intelligent woman, secular or religious, is no doubt aware of many of the rewards of mothering. Not long ago, a woman wrote an article in a professional lawyers' magazine, defending her choice to temporarily drop out of her law practice in order to raise her child. She brought all the arguments that most educated people would bring in terms of the benefits to both child and parent. A child needs the security of a loving parent who is truly there for him or her. It is satisfying to help a young child learn such things as colors, shapes, and letters. It is largely in the parents' hands to teach their child how to be happy, contributive, and a good citizen. It is rewarding to witness the child's daily growth and development. It sounded very much like what one would expect a religious Jewish woman to say. Yet being a Jewish mother has a still deeper dimension.

The descendants of Abraham are compared to the stars, each of which has its own fire and radiates its own light. Each Jewish child — indeed, every child — has a unique message to bring forth. When a woman has a spiritual worldview, she realizes that in nurturing the development of another human being she is ultimately enabling someone to bring a specific spiritual light into the world. The kind of world we live in is ultimately a result of the spirituality of the people who comprise it.

While one can give to society in innumerable ways, bringing new humans into existence and imbuing them with spiritual values ensures the perpetuation of everything that makes life worth living. It is therefore the most fundamental contribution one can make to the world.

A Jewish woman has the further consciousness of the unique role of her people in working toward a more ethical, humane, and just world for everyone. She believes that with the proper spiritual nurture her child will be able to make his or her special and meaningful contribution, however small, toward that end. This aspiration goes far beyond desiring to raise a person to be healthy, happy, and well adjusted.

Simultaneously, spiritually conscious mothering involves much more personal growth on the part of the mother. In creating the world, God directed His energies outside of Himself and, in so doing, bestowed something of Himself upon the world. Projecting one's innermost essence onto something else, whether it be a canvas, a lump of clay, or a home, is likewise the basis of all human creativity. In focusing her energies on her children, a mother projects who she is onto them. She becomes more of who she herself can be in emulating God's primary qualities of giving and nurturing life. The Hebrew word for children, *banim*, comes from the same root as the verb *banah*, build. Mothering allows a woman to directly and experientially address the aspects of herself that are most Godly and thus build herself. This can happen only if the mother has the specific spiritual awareness that a religious outlook imparts.

Practically speaking, mothering in today's society requires major reeducation. Being a mother necessitates retraining one's eye to see structure and success in situations that one sets up for oneself as opposed to situations structured by others. Finishing a report for work can bring gratification and a sense of accomplishment; so can taking a walk with a child to see the stars or taking apart an orange and examining the pieces with an interested three-year-old. As total as is the investment of self on all levels (intellectual, emotional, and so on), so are the rewards enormous.

All of this is not to say that mothering is without its trials. Many women at times find the constant physical and emotional giving involved in raising children overwhelming. The structure and camaraderie women find in external careers are often assumed to be unavailable in mothering, and thus little effort is exerted to obtain them. In many communities there is little real emotional support extended to mothers by family or friends, and women may be reluctant to request such support because they fear this suggests inadequacy. Yet nurturing does not have to be experienced in splendid isolation. Sharing and extending mutual support are not only important but necessary and usually are found to be a natural and integral part of a society that values mothering.

Orthodox Jewish families will usually have as many children as God will grant them. Depending on which segment of the religious world one observes, families of five to ten children are common. Religious Jews value souls coming into the world both for the good of each soul (which now has an opportunity to rectify and perfect itself) and for the fulfillment of the mission of the Jewish people, to which each soul is expected to contribute. Thus, Orthodox society considers "the more children, the better," just as secular society considers "the more money, the better."

No one in secular society ever complains of having too much money, even though more money requires more time, more taxes, and more responsibility. To a person who values money, it is obvious that the advantages of having more money outweigh the weight of the responsibilities entailed. Similarly, to a person who values children, the advantages of bringing as many souls into the world as possible outweigh the costs on all levels.

In the secular world, a couple's reluctance to have a large family often stems from the fear of not being able to provide each child with the quality of time and attention that will maximize his or her development as a person. Unquestionably, the day has only twenty-four hours, whether one has two children or twelve. The needs of parents to sleep, eat, and so on are not by the nature of things negotiable. This invariably takes us to the conclusion that children with many siblings get less undivided time with their parents than do only children or those with just one or two "competitors."

This observation is not necessarily valid. The Jewish people has never valued quantity over quality and clearly would advocate producing a smaller number of top-notch children over a larger number of poorly nurtured ones. Therefore, one must question why the small family, where each child has greater private access to his or her parents, was never idealized in Judaism.

There is an assumption that the environment created by large-family life can in itself be instrumental in the individual development of each child. What makes family life work, when it does, is both commitment to being contributive and valuing the contribution of each member. The dynamic created by each person being someone upon whom others count and who is appreciated by others leads to spiritual and psychological growth. Even a contribution such as bringing a diaper when asked or helping a younger sibling with homework can be part of the edifice of self-esteem that is built daily in the inner vision of the child.

The small-family setup can often create the opposite dynamic: the parents are firmly defined as the ones whose purpose is to give, while the children view themselves as open-ended recipients. At best, this leads to the need to find one's potential as a contributor only outside the family and the consequent weakening of a sense of familial closeness and commitment. At worst, it can result in selfishness and self-centeredness that remain part of the child's psyche even as an adult, making success in future relationships that require giving that much less likely.

Of course, not all large families generate enough love and appreciation to enable each child to develop his or her potential, nor does every small family generate insatiable selfishness. Each family is unique, and much is a consequence of who the parents are and how they choose to structure the family living situation. This is just one area that requires the intelligence and creativity of the mother.

Two further points bear mentioning. An additional benefit of giving on the part of children in large families is that younger children find themselves the recipients of attention not only from their parents but from older siblings. This goes a long way toward compensating for the lack of attention from which smaller children might otherwise suffer. At the same time, a younger child is undoubtedly less likely to be the victim of various neuroses stemming from an unhealthy relationship with one or both parents when he or she is exposed to a greater number of potential role models.

Today, self-absorption is seemingly more a part of our society than ever. The challenge in going against present societal norms and raising a large family is also greater than ever. Perhaps we can be inspired to meet the challenge by recognizing that human beings who are healthy and whole and who have integrated the ability to give to others are needed more than ever.

Of course, there are women who feel that they are not suited for having a large number of children or babies in close succession. In Jewish law, men are not permitted to practice birth control (because of the prohibition against spilling seed), but women are. Women who are physically or emotionally unready to bear another child can usually receive a rabbinical leniency, grounded in Jewish law, to temporarily practice birth control. Because of the high value Judaism attaches to bringing children into the world, the general attitude is that limiting family size or spacing children should not be considered for superficial reasons such as "I just don't want to be tied down (bothered, inconvenienced)" or "Three is a nice number...."

Encouragement of large families notwithstanding, Jewish law does not view women as "baby machines." Judaism particularly understands the major emotional adjustments involved in adopting a religious way of life, which leave some newly observant women feeling unready to take on all that fortune may bring their way. However, because birth control is a complicated and serious issue from many angles, any religiously committed woman who feels the need to use contraception will personally (or preferably together with her husband) discuss the matter with an expert in this area in order to receive advice specific to her case. The general rule is to be honest with oneself in appraising one's capabilities and, if the limitation is a real one, not to hesitate to seek personal legal advice.

What about Housework?

Many women, when they consider the roles of wife and mother, see not the baby's glowing smile but the perpetual piles of dishes to be washed, floors to be vacuumed, and bathrooms to be cleaned. Judaism does not glorify household chores, nor does it view them as necessarily part of a woman's spiritual calling in life. Jewish law states clearly that the woman must do housework only if the couple's financial situation does not permit hiring household help. If a husband is sufficiently well off, he must hire help to relieve his wife of her chores. If he refuses, she can bring him to a Jewish court, and he will be ordered to do so. Performing menial household tasks, therefore, is not seen as a necessary means of feminine spiritual self-expression.

It must be noted, however, that housework should nevertheless not be regarded with scorn. The priests in the Temple in Jerusalem had to perform many "menial" tasks to maintain the physical appearance and cleanliness of the Temple, yet they treasured their work, knowing that it was in essence holy. The same can be said of work done to maintain the home, which is seen as a miniature Temple in terms of its inherent sanctity. The fact that Jewish law relieves those individuals who can afford it from doing such work reflects only the reality that many women find it difficult to relate to housework on this level. They should therefore be given the opportunity to engage in other activities that will more readily yield them spiritual satisfaction.

Most men have an aspect of their lives parallel to most women's need to do housework: the need to earn a living. The obligation of the wife to assume the responsibility for household chores is parallel to the husband's obligation to provide for the full material support of his family.

Work is a curse originating from the time of Adam and Eve. The ideal situation for a man is to be independently wealthy and thus free to pursue those specific activities (particularly Torah study) that he finds spiritually growth-producing, which may or may not entail a professional career. A man for whom this rare reality does not exist must work. If he is lucky, he may find a measure of satisfaction in his job, but even the most stimulating professions include a good share of tedium.

The woman's need to do housework assumes a relationship in which the husband produces all of the family's income while the wife alone runs the home. Jewish law permits the husband and wife to make their own personal arrangement as to how these responsibilities will be shared. A couple may choose for the wife to work outside the home and for the husband to assume a share of the household chores. This, in fact, is the norm in many religious communities. Such decisions are entirely up to the couple to make in accordance with their own unique needs, desires, and abilities.

Today, while many among us can afford to pay for cleaning help at least once a week, most of our lifestyles do not include the luxury of having the baking, cooking, and laundry done by a large entourage of live-in servants. Most religious women, moreover, choose to take primary responsibility for raising their children and thus spend more time at home than their husbands. As a practical consequence of both of these realities, the responsibility for household work today falls more often not to servants or the husband but to the wife. The choice as to whether the necessity for food to be cooked, dishes to be washed, and so on will generate depression, anxiety, and feelings of imprisonment or whether it will open us to giving, caring, and creativity is our own.

A little bit of practical knowledge can go a long way toward alleviating the frustrations many young wives suffer when confronted with the task of running a home. The incredible absence of any type of simple education preparatory to finding oneself in this situation is almost unbelievable. I know intelligent women (and men) buried physically and emotionally under piles of dirty laundry and half-prepared lunches. They are as successful at homemaking as a person would be at driving a car without ever having taken driving lessons or seen a car driven.

I should know — learning to prioritize, organize, and get it all done while still having time to pursue other things was no easy task for me. Like many others, I had to figure it out the hard way during my first years of marriage. My early adventures included almost killing myself when someone was helping me clean my oven by using a mixture of bleach and ammonia in an attempt to dislodge the grease. (The fumes! The hysteria!)

Looking back, I realize that for most of us there is nothing inherently fulfilling about housework. Still, it is somewhat ridiculous to assume that in a society where people must cook, it is more important to know *The Career of President Millard Fillmore: Its Rise and Fall* than how to clean an oven without killing oneself.

Jewish Singlehood

Many women who very much want to marry find themselves waiting a long time before they succeed in finding the right husband. While there are countless avenues through which such women can continue to develop themselves spiritually, during this time they often experience the feeling of existing in limbo and of lacking a framework for further growth. Yet while being alone can be a very painful state, to waste the pain in a choice not to move on translates singlehood into an unnecessary tragedy.

A single woman is in a unique position in that she can focus more strongly on developing and nurturing particular aspects of her spiritual self. She has more opportunity for prayer, meditation, and study than one whose time is more committed. If her inclinations tend toward the less ethereal, she may find that she can put her abilities and talents to use in becoming a community giver, a role Jewish women have played since time immemorial. Whether this giving involves volunteering, teaching, organizing, or opening one's heart to the lonely, the potential for self-development is tremendous.

Although all the major Jewish figures in the Bible indeed married at some point, many narratives of the lives of biblical women do not relate directly to who they were in marriage but to their individuality in a broader sense. They can thus provide insight into how a woman can grow irrespective of her marital status.

I would suggest that one study the lives of Ruth and Naomi (from *Megillat Ruth*). Naomi experienced her time of most significant spiritual growth after she had been widowed in Moab. She had the fortitude to go back to the Land of Israel, despite the shame of letting people who had known her as a wealthy woman now see her destitute.

When people asked, "Is this Naomi?" she replied, "Don't call me Naomi" (which means pleasant, as her previous life had been), "but call me Marah" (bitter, as her life had become) "because God has dealt thus with me."

Formerly wealthy, she saw the loss of her husband and two sons, as well as her poverty, as part of divine justice because the family left the Land of Israel in a time of famine instead of remaining to aid the community. Instead of being embittered and angry at God, she looked within herself to see what she could learn from the course her life had taken, and the consequent spiritual growth she experienced was tremendous.

When you consider Ruth, who also discovered the deepest part of herself, not during her first marriage, but after she was widowed, you can trace how she developed the qualities of kindness, truth, and internality. Her personal development and ability to meet challenges are an inspiration to any woman, not only to one who is faced with difficulties.

These are lives that show us true womanhood.

Esther (of *Megillat Esther*, the Purim story) and Rachav (of the book of Joshua, chapter 2) are further examples. Esther had the ability to find grace in the eyes of all who saw her. On a deep level, this means that she could find and draw forth the Godliness in all people to whom she addressed herself, whether King Ahasuerus or her serving women. The Midrash relates that Esther's serving women, deeply inspired by the way she dealt with them, actually converted to Judaism. This is a spiritual skill that has nothing to do with marriage.

Rachav, the Canaanite woman who helped the Israelites conquer Jericho, evolved from being sunken in the immorality of Canaanite culture to reaching a level of holiness that made her worthy of marrying Joshua, the leader of the Jewish people after Moses' death. Because she allowed herself to be moved by news of what God had done for the Israelites, she abandoned her entire way of thinking and being. Her openness to new ideas, and her willingness to put herself on the line for them, gave her the courage to hide the Israelite spies in her home. Her personal growth preceded her marriage to Joshua.

Finally, there is the ideal Jewish woman as portrayed and immortalized in King Solomon's poem, *A Woman of Valor*. While she is both a wife and mother, and a significant portion of the poem refers to her as such, many of the praises sung about her could be sung as well for any childless or unmarried woman who is conscious of her spiritual capacity in various areas. She is described as being industrious, resourceful, nurturing and kind, entrepreneurial, courageous, charitable, majestic, wise, and deeply religious.

Her children and husband laud her, but, most important, she herself is aware of her worth and the significance of her contributions. (To fully explore in depth the varied aspects of the woman of valor, please refer to my book *More Precious than Pearls: Selected Insights into the Qualities of the Ideal Woman*.) Suffice it to say that such a woman, in representing the paradigm of female spiritual accomplishment, serves as the ideal role model for all Jewish women, married or single.

Of course, many fine (and more accessible) role models also exist in the communities in which we live today. A dear friend of mine, divorced and childless, showed just how far one can go in developing one's talents and ability to contribute to others while unmarried. She studied the Russian language and became unquestionably the most successful woman teacher in the underground Jewish schools of pre-glasnost Russia. (That she eventually found her new husband there is, of course, icing on the cake!) This is just one modern-day example of a woman who achieved enormous spiritual growth, as well as personal satisfaction in life, while single.

Conclusion

The best possible result that reading a book such as this could bring about is the desire to ask more questions. If we have learned nothing else by experiencing the events of the last century, we have learned to question widely held assumptions and to take responsibility for our own lives.

Many of the questions brought under discussion here are, in the end, only partially answered. If you are Jewish and feel you want to further explore these and other issues, an extensive list of organizations, institutions, and individuals in North America, Israel, and throughout the world, who will be able to direct you in further Jewish learning, can be found in *The Jewish Travelers' Resource Guide* (compiled by Jeffrey Seidel). The guide can be obtained by contacting the Jewish Student Information Center, at 17 Shonei Halachot, Old City, Jerusalem, Israel, or jseidel@jeffseidel.com (www.jeffseidel.com), or by phone at 9722-628-2634 or fax at 9722-628-8338.

The beauty of the lifestyle described here may seem to deserve a second glance. Looking twice sometimes enriches the first glance and opens new perspectives. Enjoy!

NOTES

One: Feminism or Masculism?

p. 1. *To quote Naomi Wolf*: Naomi Wolf, *Misconceptions: Truth, Lies, and the Unexpected on the Journey to Motherhood*.

p. 3. *his poem A Woman of Valor*: Proverbs 31:10–31.

p. 4. *"Feminism," as quickly as it gained momentum*: See, for example, Mary Ann Mason, *The Equality Trap* (New York: Simon & Schuster, 1990).

p. 7. *Gloria Steinem's wry and accurate observation*: "If Men Could Menstruate," *Ms. Magazine*, October 1978, p. 110.

Two: Acknowledging Differences

p. 10. *"The Brain That's Lame"*: Edgar F. Berman, *The Compleat Chavinist*.

p. 10. *"Men versus Dogs"*: Barbara Lovehouse, *No Bad Men* (New American Library, 1984).

p. 10. *According to Jewish tradition*: Eruvin 18a.

p. 10. *"Male and female He created them"*: Genesis 5:2.

p. 11. *The original Adam was totally self-sufficient:* Nachmanides to Genesis 2:18.

p. 11. *"It is not good for Adam to be alone"*: Genesis 2:18.

p. 11. *The first is that total independence*: Rashi to Genesis 2:18.

p. 11. *The world was created so that God*: Psalms 89:3; *Tanya*, Part 2, ch. 4.

p. 11. *Both men and women were created*: Genesis 1:27.

p. 12. *The male-female polarity is thus essential*: ibid.

p. 12. *An article in Newsweek entitled "Guns and Dolls"*: May 28, 1990, p. 56.

p. 13. *The first person, the Torah tells us*: Genesis 2:7.

p. 13. *Woman is described as being built*: Genesis 2:21. While *Rashi* interprets *tzela* as "side," *Siftei Chachamim* explains that the simple meaning is "rib." (Had only the meaning "side" been intended, the word *tzad* could have been used.)

p. 13. *Woman is to be the internal*: See Genesis Rabbah 18:2.

p. 15. *An individual woman may have*: See Maimonides, *Hilchot Talmud Torah*. 1:13, where the expression "most women" acknowledges the reality of exceptions.

p. 16. *Judaism views all physical reality*: *Sha'arei Kedushah* 1:1.

p. 16. *In reference to humans, this means*: Ibid.

p. 16. *"Let us make the human"*: Genesis 1:26.

p. 16. *Rashi, the foremost biblical commentator*: Rashi to Genesis 1:26.

p. 17. *"In our image" Rashi explains*: Ibid.

p. 17. *meaning that we are in a sense*: See *Siftei Chachachim* to *Rashi* above.

p. 17. *God Himself has no physical form*: One may therefore wonder why God is most often referred to as "He." Jewish mysticism recognizes that God has both masculine and feminine aspects. Those characterized as giving forth or acting upon the world (creation, rulership, etc.) are described as masculine, while those which entail receptivity (as with offerings, etc.) are described as feminine. In our daily lives we more often have cause to relate to God as a giver, so we generally refer to Him in the masculine. (Hebrew has no generic personal pronoun.)

p. 17. *Each limb and organ of the body*: *Sha'arei Kedushah* 1:1.

p. 17. *In rabbinic literature, the commandments*: *Zohar, Vayishlach* 102.

p. 17. *the three cognitive emanations*: For more, see Aryeh Kaplan, *Innerspace* (Jerusalem: Moznaim, 1990).

p. 18. *God made most men*: Maharal, *Tiferet Yisrael* 56.

p. 18. *"Say this to the house of Jacob"*: Exodus 19:3.

p. 18. *Our sages note that "house of Jacob"*: *Rashi* to above.

p. 19. *Woman tend, however*: See, for example, Baba Metzia 59a; Moed Katan 9b.

p. 20. *The Torah notes that the first woman*: Genesis 2:18.

p. 20. *She was later given the name Chavah*: Genesis 3:20.

p. 20. *Women's heightened consciousness*: See, for example, Kiddushin 41a; Ruth Rabbah 2; Tosefta Ketubot 12:3.

p. 20. *"active participants in the development of others"*: Jean Baker Miller, *Toward a New Psychology of Women*, 2nd ed. (Boston: Beacon Press, 1986).

p. 20. *women perceive their very sense of self*: Jean Baker Miller and Carol Gilligan, *In a Different Voice* (Cambridge, MA: Harvard University Press, 1982).

p. 20. *the female libido is less likely*: Jerusalem Talmud Ketubot 5:8; Ketubot 64b.

p. 21. *women are less prone to physical aggression*: Kiddushin 2b; Yevamot 65b.

p. 21. *Most men develop spiritual consciousness*: Maharal, *Netiv HaEmunah*, ch.1 (near end).

p. 21. *Most women's primary source*: Ibid.

p. 21. *more precisely defined as trust*: Ibid. (2nd paragraph).

p. 22. *Preparatory to entering the Land of Israel*: Numbers 13.

p. 22. *The women, however, guided by trust*: Sifri, *Pinchas* 133.

p. 22. *Hence the Torah says that during the battle*: Exodus 17:12.

p. 22. *Therefore, the earliest Aramaic translation*: *Targum* to above.

Three: Power: Public and Private

p. 28. *Sarah understood the negative*: Genesis 21:9–10 and *Rashi* thereon.

p. 28. *"In all that Sarah says to you"*: Genesis 21:12.

p. 28. *Commentators on this verse*: Rashi (as well as others) to above.

p. 28. *Rebecca also clearly intuited*: Genesis 27:1–40.

p. 28. *The Sages of the Talmud*: Sotah 11b.

p. 30. *Carol Gilligan, noted researcher*: In a Different Voice (see notes to p. 20).

p. 32. *For example, there must be two witnesses*: Hirsch to Deuteronomy 17:6.

p. 32. *They must have seen one another*: Maimonides, Hilchot Edut 4:1.

p. 32. *If a third person*: Ibid. 5:3.

p. 32. *There is a category of people*: Shevuot 42a; Baba Kama 106b; Baba Batra 155b.

p. 32. *relatives of the plaintiff or defendant*: Maimonides, *Hilchot Melachim* 13:15.

p. 32. *kings*: Ibid., 3:7.

p. 32. *Tosafot, a leading Talmudic commentator*: to Zevachim 103a s.v. *Ein*.

p. 32. *In legal matters in which*: Maimonides, *Hilchot Sanhedrin* 24:1.

p. 32. *Even in cases requiring witnesses*: *Choshen Mishpat* 25:14.

p. 38. *only someone who is obligated*: Mishnah, Rosh HaShanah 3:8.

p. 38. *that women do not serve*: Deborah was permitted to be a national leader of the Jewish people only because she was thus instructed through prophecy (Ridbaz to Maimonides, *Hilchot Melachim* 1:5).

p. 38. *In spending most of her time*: Genesis 18:9 and 21:12 and *Rashi* thereon.

p. 38. *That this constitutes the ideal form of prayer*: Samuel I 1:12–13.

p. 40. *The text reports seventy "souls"*: Genesis 46:6–27. One of the seventy named is actually a woman, Dinah (verse 15). Dinah is mentioned not as the inner but the outer half (see ahead in text), since she never assumed the more internal role due to the tragic circumstances of her life (Genesis 34).

p. 40. *The resolution of this discrepancy*: Exodus 1:1.

p. 40. *He is the external force*: Megillah 23b. Accordingly, tribal affiliation and priesthood (communal roles) are determined through patrilineal descent, while Jewish identity (essence) is bestowed through the mother. Likewise, a man is called to the Torah as the son of his father, while we pray for someone as the son or daughter of his or her mother.

p. 41. *Thus, in the commandment of lighting*: Mishnah Berurah 9 to *Shulchan Aruch, Orach Chaim* 675:3. A woman who wishes to light for herself may do so (*Rama* to *Shulchan Aruch, Orach Chaim* 671:2).

p. 42. *The Talmud states that "one hundred women"*: Berachot 45b.

p. 42. *a woman is permitted...to make the blessing over wine*: *Shulchan Aruch, Orach Chaim* 271:2.

p. 42. *and to read the megillah*: Mishnah Berurah to *Shulchan Aruch, Orach Chaim* 689:1.

p. 42. *if it is at all possible*: Mishnah Berurah to *Shulchan Aruch, Orach Chaim* 271:4; *Shulchan Aruch, Orach Chaim* 689:2.

p. 43. *The Talmud states that it is not*: Megillah 23a.

Four: What You See Is What You Get: The Laws of Modesty

p. 49. *throughout history men have sexually exploited*: Ketubot 64b.

p. 51. *Tzniut is a consciousness that the Torah*: Micah 6:9.

p. 51. *Primarily, women are acknowledged*: Genesis Rabbah 18:2.

p. 53. *Publicly projecting oneself in such a way*: Sifri 258 (to Deuteronomy 23:16).

p. 53. *sleeves to the elbows*: Berachot 24a.

p. 53. *skirts below the knee*: ibid.

p. 53. *necklines to the collarbone*: Mishnah Berurah to *Shulchan Aruch, Orach Chaim* 75:2.

p. 54. *In the hallowed realm of relations*: Ketubot 48a.

p. 55. *The Bible states that when the leadership*: Exodus 4:14.

p. 55. *Jewish law does not generally permit*: See *Responsa Yaskil Avdi, Yoreh Dei'ah* Dei'ah 20; *Responsa Yabia Omer* 6, *Yoreh Dei'ah* 14:7.

p. 55. *the Torah forbids either sex*: Deuteronomy 22:5.

p. 55. *The unisex image*: See Maimonides, *Sefer HaMitzvot*, negative precept #2.

p. 56. *many rabbinical opinions*: See *Prisha* to *Tur* 182:5 (first explanation); *Responsa Yabia Omer* 6, *Yoreh Dei'ah* 14:7.

p. 56. *In circumstances where*: See *Responsa Avnei Tzedek, Yoreh Dei'ah* 72.

p. 56. *One of the laws of modesty*: *Shulchan Aruch, Even HaEzer* 21:1; *Iggrot Moshe, Even HaEzer* 1:58.

p. 56. *That hair is viewed*: See Maimonides, *Hilchot Issurei Biah* 21:2.

p. 56. *The fact that divorced and widowed women*: See *Iggrot Moshe, Even HaEzer* 1:57.

p. 57. *covering her hair serves*: This idea has been suggested by Rabbi Daniel Shiloh, cited in Elyakim Ellinson, *Hatzne'a Lechet*, 2nd ed. (Jerusalem: World Zionist Organization, Department for Education and Culture in the Diaspora, 1981), p. 96. (English edition: *The Modest Way*.)

p. 57. *many modern authorities do permit them*: See *Iggrot Moshe, Even HaEzer* 2:12; *Yaskil Avdi* 7, *Even HaEzer* 16.

p. 57. *The Torah prohibits women*: *Shulchan Aruch, Even HaEzer* 21:1.

p. 58. *through the singing voice*: Metzudat David to Song of Songs 2:14.

p. 58. *Music has always been recognized*: See, for example, Allen Bloom, *The Closing of the American Mind* (New York: Simon & Schuster, 1987), p. 68ff.

p. 58. *the singing voice is viewed as a source of sensual attraction*: Berachot 24a.

p. 58. *when fused with the visual*: Sotah 48a; Maharam Shik *Even HaEzer* 53.

p. 58. *men as a group tend to respond*: Sanhedrin 75a.

p. 58. *The Torah therefore prohibits a man*: *Sefer Chasidim* (late twelfth century) likewise prohibits a woman from hearing a man sing.

p. 59. *Men are prohibited from looking*: Numbers 15:39 and Sifri 115. Men are not permitted, given a viable alternative, to go to places where they will inevitably see exposed women (Baba Batra 57b; *Aruch HaShulchan* 24:1; *Iggrot Moshe, Even HaEzer* 1:56).

p. 59. *Even a man's permission to look*: Shabbat 64b; Eruvin 18b; Avodah Zarah 20a; *Iggrot Moshe, Orach Chayim* 40, *Even HaEzer* 56.

p. 60. *It is good to be able to help*: Leviticus 19:14.

p. 61. *a certain type of strength and fearlessness*: Maharal, *Netivot Olam, Netiv HaTzniut*, ch.1.

Five: The Spiritual Path of Jewish Women

p. 64. *Indeed, the Talmud tells us*: Genesis Rabbah 45:5.

p. 65. *Although according to many major poskim*: *Rashi* and *Tosefot* to Berachot 20b; Nachmanides, *Hasagot LeSefer HaMitzvot* 5; *Mishnah Berurah* 106:4.

p. 65. *all rabbinic opinions agree*: Berachot 20b; Maimonides, *Sefer Ahavah* 1:2; *Sefer HaMitzvot*, positive mitzvah #5.

p. 68. *The ideal state for a person*: *Shulchan Aruch, Orach Chaim* 95:11.

p. 68. *Praying outdoors, for example*: Maimonides, *Hilchot Tefillah* 5.

p. 68. *In the synagogue, mirrors*: *Shulchan Aruch, Orach Chaim* 90:202; *Mishnah Berurah* thereon, par. 22.

p. 69. *three are regarded as specific*: Genesis Rabbah 17:8.

p. 69. *That is, while both men and women*: *Mishnah Berurah* to *Shulchan Aruch, Orach Chaim* 263.

p. 69. *The Torah narrates that when Isaac married Rebecca*: Genesis 24:67.

p. 70. *the three miracles that were present*: Genesis Rabbah 60:17.

p. 70. *The three miracles that occurred*: Maharal, *Gur Aryeh* to Genesis 24:67.

p. 70. *These three precepts also bear a direct relation*: Genesis Rabbah 17:8.

p. 70. *The Garden of Eden narrative*: Genesis 3.

p. 71. *"Let them make for Me a sanctuary"*: Exodus 25:8.

p. 71. *Note that the original commandment*: See *Seforno* to above.

p. 71. *The Tabernacle was meant to be*: *Malbim* to beginning of *Parashat Trumah* (Exodus 25), in section *Rimazei HaMishkan*, citing Maimonides, *Guide to the Perplexed*, ch. 72, part 1.

p. 71. *Each detail of the Temple's physical structure*: See *Malbim* above; Hirsch to *Parashat Trumah* (Exodus 25–27).

p. 72. *This bread, like Sarah's, stayed fresh*: Pesachim 46b.

p. 73. *The Talmud states that in the absence*: Menachot 93a.

p. 73. *A man's work traditionally consists*: Yevamot 63a.

p. 73. *"I will greatly increase your anguish"*: Genesis 3:16.

p. 74. *The human soul is called God's candle*: Proverbs 20:27.

p. 74. *Looked at simply, the lighting*: Shabbat 23b.

p. 74. *The Shabbat is referred to metaphorically as a bride*: "Lechah Dodi," liturgy for Shabbat evening.

p. 74. *or a queen*: Baba Kama 32a.

p. 75. *Both of these feminine images*: Maharal, *Tiferet Yisrael*, ch. 40.

p. 75. *These emotional challenges can lead*: See *Iggrot Moshe, Yorah Dei'ah* 103.

p. 75. *The moment of candle lighting*: See *Mishnah Berurah* to *Shulchan Aruch, Orach Chaim* 263:1.

p. 75. *The custom of praying at the time*: Shabbat 23b.

p. 76. *Rabbi Aryeh Kaplan in The Waters of Eden*: Second edition (New York: National Congregation of Synagogue Youth, 1982), pp. 40–41.

p. 76. *Judaism considers everything about the body*: Sha'arei Kedushah 1:1.

p. 76. *Even such a simple fact*: Maharal, *Netivot Olam, Netiv HaLashon*, ch. 3.

p. 76. *The need for this consciousness*: Genesis Rabbah 17:18.

p. 76. *by allowing a subjective vision*: Maimonides, *Guide to the Perplexed*, ch. 2. See also Shraga Silverstein, *The Antidote* (Jerusalem: Feldheim Publishers, 1979), particularly ch. 2.

p. 77. *The best translation for it*: See Aryeh Kaplan, cited above.

p. 77. *The ultimate blockage is death*: Ibid.

p. 78. *This Presence is the aspect of God*: *Tanya*, Part I, ch. 33.

p. 78. *It is described as God's feminine aspect*: Ibid.

p. 79. *The commentators tell us that Abraham*: Genesis Rabbah 56:2 (to Genesis 22:4).

p. 79. *God's Presence represents itself*: Maharal, *Gur Aryeh* to Genesis 24:67.

p. 79. *One of the Torah's decrees*: Leviticus 19:2.

p. 79. *Holiness in its classical sense*: Nachmanides, *Kedoshim* 4.

p. 80. *The Midrash relates that Eve*: Zohar, *Bereishit*, 2:202 and following.

p. 80. *"To your husband shall be your desire"*: Genesis 3:16.

p. 80. *This, say the commentators, refers*: *Rashi* to above; Eruvin 100b.

p. 81. *It therefore alleviates the frustration*: The mitzvah which more directly and comprehensively addresses this problem is *onah*, which commands a man to be attuned and respond to his wife's intimations of desire.

p. 82. *The function of presenting a sacrifice*: Nachmanides to Leviticus 1:2–4. See

Hirsch on the entire topic of sacrifices.

p. 84. *The Talmud states that the physical*: Niddah 31b.

p. 84. *Bird offerings were generally offered*: Hirsch to Leviticus 1:17.

p. 85. *The sacrifice of a bird offering*: Ibid. and to 12:6.

p. 85. *In terms of the negative commandments*: Kiddushin 35a.

p. 86. *The positive commandments aimed specifically at men*: See Maimonides, *Sefer HaMitzvot*, end of positive mitzvot.

p. 86. *such voluntary performance is considered meritorious*: See, for example, Maimonides, *Hilchot Talmud Torah* 1:13 (although the study of Talmud, from which women are exempt, is not a positive time-bound commandment).

p. 86. *When women accept such an optional precept*: *Magen Avraham* to *Shulchan Aruch, Orach Chaim* 489:1.

p. 86. *An example of this*: See *Chayei Adam, Hilchot Rosh HaShanah* 141:7.

p. 87. *The few commandmants that are not open*: See Moshe Meiselman, *Jewish Woman in Jewish Law* (New York: Ktav, 1978), ch. 21–22 on tallit and tefillin. Some authorities do permit women to observe these precepts.

p. 87. *That men are obligated*: *Tosafot* to Menachot 44a, s.v. *zil tefei*.

p. 88. *Men, therefore, when saying*: For a psychological perspective on the purpose of these three blessings, see Moshe HaLevi Spero, "The Didactic-Psychological Function of Three Rabbinic Blessings," *Proceedings of the Association of Orthodox Jewish Scientists* (New York: Sepher-Herman Press, 1897), vol. 8–9, pp. 111–146.

p. 89. *The biblical story of Rebecca*: Genesis 24:17–20 ff.

p. 91. *As Maimonides said*: Hilchot Dei'ot 3:23 through end of chapter.

p. 92. *the medieval classic Duties of the Heart*: Rabbi Bachya Ibn Pekudah, Part I, *Sha'ar HaBitachon*, pp. 227–228 in the Warsaw Goldman Press edition.

p. 94. *the commandment to sanctify the new moon*: Exodus 12:1.

p. 94. *The Midrash tells us*: *Sefat Emet* #658.

p. 95. *Emunah (trust), the strong sense*: Sotah 11b.

p. 95. *We are told that we were saved*: Mechilta on *Parashat Bo*, para. 5.

p. 95. *The same faith prevented*: Pirkei DeRabbi Eliezer 45 to Exodus 32:2–3.

p. 95. *Moses was on Mount Sinai*: Rashi to Exodus 31:1; rest of chapter.

p. 95. *In the merit of their faith*: Tur to *Shulchan Aruch, Orach Chaim* 417.

p. 96. *Women could almost be considered*: See Shabbat 62a. While the reference here is to attire, the statement can be understood more generally.

p. 96. *Sisterhood is epitomized in the Torah*: Exodus 1:15–21.

p. 97. *In every age and in every country*: See Shoshana Pantel Zolty, *And All Your Childen Shall Be Learned* (New York: Jason Aronson, Inc., 1993).

p. 99. *In terms of spiritual direction, such study*: While neither the Talmud nor the *rishonim* cite women being less strong in *da'at* as a reason for their exemption from studying Talmud, later sources do. See Maimondes, *Hilchot Talmud Torah* 1:13; *Torah Temimah* to Deuteronomy 11:19, #48.

p. 99. *Maimonides's four conditions: Hilchot Dei'ot* 6:6–7.

p. 100. *Today especially, formal education for girls*: Chafetz Chaim, *Likutei Halachot, Sotah* 21; *Moznayim LeMishpat* 1:42.

p. 100. *He states that in times*: *Moznayim LeMishpat* 1:42.

p. 100. *If it is clear that such a woman*: See *Torah Temimah* cited above, quoting *Ma'ayan Ganim*.

p. 100. *For whatever a woman chooses*: Maimonides, *Hilchot Talmud Torah* 1:13.

p. 100. *If a man (even her father) implies*: ibid.

p. 101. *Another reason for separate education*: See *Iggrot Moshe, Yorah Dei'ah* 1:137.

Six: Marriage

p. 103. *The first commandment that God gave Adam*: Genesis 1:28.

p. 103. *They must marry and produce*: *Sefer HaChinuch* #1.

p. 103. *Jewish women are not obligated*: Yevamot 61b; Maimonides, *Hilchot Ishut* 15:16; Yevamot 65b.

p. 103. *"paths are paths of pleasantness"*: Proverbs 3:17.

p. 103. *would not command a woman*: *Meshech Chochmah* to Genesis 9:7.

p. 105. *At the time of woman's creation*: *Targum Yonatan* to Genesis 2:15; Kiddushin 82a. See Genesis 3:10, 17–18.

p. 105. *After Adam and Eve made their fatal mistake*: Genesis 2:17–18.

p. 105. *Clearly, much of the giving within marriage*: *Kli Yakar* to Genesis 2:18.

p. 106. *"Her husband is known"*: Proverbs 31:23.

p. 107. *Acquisition in this case*: See, for example, Exodus 15:16; *Pirkei Avot* 6:10. In both cases *kinyan* refers to bonding.

p. 107. *the man has the final word*: Baba Metzia 59a.

p. 108. *woman is in charge of*: Ibid. This division of authority is not, however, halachically mandated.

p. 108. *While men may have*: See *Zohar, Terumah* 166, on *"ner mitzvah veTorah or."*

p. 108. *Men are told explicitly in the Talmud*: Baba Metzia 59a.

p. 108. *"A proper wife does the will"*: Tanna DeVei Eliyahu, Seder Eliyahu Rabbah 10. See also Maimonides, *Hilchot Ishah* 15:20. These admonitions, however, do not have halachic force.

p. 109. *A person's deepest will is identical*: Maimonides, *Hilchot Gerushin* 2:20.

p. 109. *The idea that ultimately people want*: Me'orei Or 90:20.

p. 109. *"If he is worthy," says Rashi*: to Genesis 2:18.

p. 110. *On the other hand, in the Garden of Eden*: Genesis 3:1.

p. 110. *on the assumption that she would be*: Rashi to Genesis 3:15.

p. 110. *well-known story in the Midrash*: Genesis Rabbah 17:7.

p. 111. *On a psychological level, it has been noted*: See Baker Miller and Gilligan (notes to p. 20), and Nancy Chodorow, *The Reproduction of Mothering* (Berkeley, CA: University of California Press, 1978).

p. 112. *Indeed, numerous Jewish books*: See, for example, Aharon Feldman, *The River, the Kettle and the Bird* (Jerusalem: CBS Publications, 1987), ch. 5–6.

p. 112. *oft-quoted maxim from Pirkei Avot*: 1:14.

p. 114. *According to the Torah, the sin of adultery*: Maimonides, *Hilchot Yesodei HaTorah* 5:10.

p. 115. *while this is forbidden*: Maimonides, *Hilchot Issurei Biah* 1. *Sefer HaChinuch*, mitzvah #570, states the prohibition on a man having relations with a woman without *kiddushin* and *ketubah* (i.e., marriage).

p. 115. *This breach is so severe*: Maharal, *Tiferet Yisrael*, ch. 36.

p. 115. *The Torah describes a specific process*: Numbers 5:11–31.

p. 116. *it became forbidden for her*: Sotah 6a.

p. 116. *The woman was given ample opportunity*: Sotah 8a.

p. 116. *The entire narrative starts with the premise*: Sotah 6a.

p. 116. *symbolizing that she had given in*: Hirsch to Numbers 5:17–21.

p. 117. *At any point in the process thus far*: Sotah 19a.

p. 117. *This was meant to convey*: Ibid.

p. 117. *This fate was simultaneously experienced*: Sotah 57b. The waters worked only if her husband was "clean from sin," i.e., hadn't had relations with any forbidden women.

p. 117. *an individual's accountability for sin*: For example, after Moses, the greatest prophet who ever lived, performed an action which reflected a tiny flaw in his belief in God, he was not permitted to enter the Land of Israel.

p. 117. *According to Jewish law, a man*: Shulchan Aruch, Even HaEzer 26:4, 27:1.

p. 118. *When they marry, he presents her*: Levush 66:1.

p. 118. *A woman does not present a man*: Iggrot Moshe, Even HaEzer 3:18.

p. 118. *general nature of legal contracting*: See Moshe Meiselman, *Jewish Woman in Jewish Law* (New York: Ktav, 1978), pp. 97–98.

p. 118. *the understanding of the man as*: Deuteronomy 22:13; Kiddushin 2b.

p. 119. *The enactment of the divorce*: Shulchan Aruch, Even HaEzer 120:1, 133:1, 136:1.

p. 119. *(although it is forbidden and grounds for divorce)*: *Sefer HaChinuch*, mitzvah #570 states the prohibition on a man having relations with a woman without *kiddushin* and *ketubah* (i.e., marriage). Today, a married man who has relations with a woman who is not his wife is regarded as a person of low character, which many rabbis deem grounds for divorce. Rav Ephraim Oshry in

She'eilot UT'shuvot MiMa'amakim rules that even if a man believes he is a widower and remarries, if his first wife is later found to be alive, he must divorce his second wife.

p. 119. *nor can a man toss his wife*: The ban on divorcing a woman against her will is included in the Ban of Rabbeinu Gershom.

p. 121. *"heter mei'ah rabbanim"*: This was enacted simultaneously with the ban on polygyny (see above).

p. 123. *"feminization of poverty"*: See Mary Ann Mason, *The Equality Trap* (notes to p. 4); "The Failure of Feminism," *Newsweek*, November 9, 1990, p. 9.

p. 124. *"Where there is a rabbinic will"*: Blu Greenberg, Jewish feminist leader.

p. 124. *One of the commandments is to obey*: *Sefer HaChinuch*, mitzvah #475.

p. 126. *Such a man could, upon leaving*: Maimonides, *Hilchot Gerushin* ch. 8–11; Shabbat 56a; Ketubot 9b.

p. 126. *the Talmud adopted various leniences*: Yevamot 87b, 88a.

p. 126. *In certain cases, a marriage*: Ketubot 2b, 3a.

p. 127. *formula for a prenuptial agreement*: Regarding prenuptial agreements, one should follow the recommendations of his or her rabbi.

p. 128. *the question we ask at the traditional Passover meal*: Passover Haggadah.

p. 128. *This twofold dipping alludes*: Maharal, *Gevurot Hashem* on the Passover Haggadah, on the words *"zecher lemikdash keHillel"* and *"mah nishtanah."*

Seven: Motherhood

p. 132. *The letters of the Hebrew root word*: Maharal, *Tiferet Yisrael*, ch. 34.

p. 132. Yet *Deborah herself, in the song*: Judges 5:7.

p. 133. *The descendants of Abraham are compared*: Genesis 22:17.

p. 133. *In creating the world, God directed*: *Michtav MeEliyahu*, vol. 3, p. 270.

p. 134. *The Hebrew word for children*: Genesis 16:2 and Hirsch thereon.

p. 135. *Orthodox Jewish families will usually*: The issue has not been unavailability or blanket impermissibility of contraception, as Jewish women knew about and practiced various birth control methods at least two thousand years ago.

p. 137. *In Jewish law, men are not permitted to practice*: *Sefer HaChinuch*, mitzvah #1.

p. 137. *but women are*: above.

p. 137. *the high value Judaism attaches*: See Yevamot 63b; *Sefer HaChinuch* #1.

p. 138. *the general attitude is*: *Iggrot Moshe, Even HaEzer* 63, 113 (especially end).

p. 138. *Jewish law states clearly*: *Shulchan Aruch, Even HaEzer* 80:6–10.

p. 138. *If a husband is sufficiently well-off*: Ibid., 80.

p. 139. *It must be noted, however, that housework*: See Sarah Chana Radcliffe, *Akeres HaBayis* (Southfield, MI: Targum Press, 1991).

p. 139. *The priests in the Temple in Jerusalem*: Exodus 27–30.

p. 139. *the home, which is seen as a miniature Temple*: Menachot 93a.

p. 139. *The obligation of the wife to assume*: Shulchan Aruch, Even HaEzer 69.

p. 140. *Work is a curse originating from the time*: Genesis 3:17-19.

p. 140. *Jewish law permits the husband and wife*: Shulchan Aruch, Even HaEzer 69:6.

p. 140. *A little bit of practical knowledge*: See, for example, Sarah Chana Radcliffe, *Akeres HaBayis*, cited above.

p. 142. *When people asked, "Is this Naomi?"*: Ruth, 1:19–21.

p. 143. *Esther had the ability to find grace*: Esther Rabbah to Esther 2:15.

p. 143. *On a deep level, this means*: Maharal, *Or Chadash* to Esther 2:15.

p. 143. *The Midrash relates that Esther's serving women*: Targum Esther 4:6.

p. 143. *reaching a level of holiness that made her worthy*: Megillah 14b.

p. 143. *King Solomon's poem, A Woman of Valor*: Proverbs 31:10–31.